The Ripple Effect

(Short Stories of Karma and Connection)

Deepa

AF518743

BlueRose ONE.com
Stories Matter
NewDelhi • London

BLUEROSE PUBLISHERS
India | U.K.

BlueRose ONE
Stories Matter
NewDelhi • London

For permissions requests or inquiries regarding this publication, please contact:

BLUEROSE PUBLISHERS
www.BlueRoseONE.com
info@bluerosepublishers.com
+91 8882 898 898
+4407342408967

ISBN: 978-93-6261-097-3

Cover Design: Sadhna Kumari
Typesetting: Pooja Sharma

First Edition: June 2024

YESSSSSSS...... AAI, WE DID IT;

FINALLY, OUR DREAM IS COMING TRUE. I wish you were still breathing to bless this book.

DEDICATED TO MY READERS. THIS IS WRITTEN WITH MY WHOLE HEART AND SOUL JUST FOR YOU. PLACING MY FIRST PIECE OF WRITING IN YOUR HANDS, JUST LIKE A BHAKTA OFFERING FLOWERS AT THE FEET OF HIS BELOVED LORD.

BADE BABA I KNOW YOU HAVE PLANTED PEOPLE IN MY LIFE SO I HAVE REACHED HERE TODAY.

" OM MAMAH SHIVAY"

ACKNOWLEDGEMENT

Firstly, I want to express my gratitude to my AAI and BABA. It's because of your love and trust that I am what I am today. Even if I can't see you, I know you still exist in me. That gives me strength. Aai your dream of writing the book is finally completed. I know you must be smiling up above there.

Mukund P. patil, a man of few words my husband, his silence is my encouragement{lol}. Thanks, hubby, for supporting me and being busy with your own work, that gave me a lot of free time to write the book, and less time to babysit an adult {lol}. Shourya patil, my son, no, my boss who checked on my progress. He was interested in knowing what I was writing, how much I finished. Also in between he wanted me to learn how to play roblox so that I don't get tired. Pumpum my 4-legged dachshund, thanks for being awake with me at odd hours, my constant companion on sleepless nights.

Special thanks to my brother and sisters and all those who call me maa, its your trust in me that I have decided to carry forward aai's dream, without your love and support I would never believe in myself.

Reyyyyyy (ANGEL)...... thanks for inspiring me to write the book, without you this writing would have always remained in my bucket list only. You gave me wings to fly and confidence to fly HIGHER.

And special thanks to PARVATHY BAUL JI for her blessings.

FOREWORD

I have to think carefully about the structure of the sentences before I start writing an article. However, I was immediately struck by how straightforward Deepali's language was when I started reading her stories. That moved me deeply. Her writing was naturally gifted, and I could never write as well as her.

Readers will surely love the assortment of stories in her book, Ripple Effect. Her tales always evoke strong feelings in the reader. A few of the chapters have some lovely dialogue. There are amorous chats between Deb and Aarashi in Soul Mates, a serious conversation between Nandini and Neev in Sayonee - II, and subjects worth reading about in the Laxmi-Vishnu heavenly conversations in the story Greed.

I would all be really appreciative as a reader if she could pen a few more compelling true-life human interest stories for her next book.

Best wishes.

P. Burman,

Senior journalist

ABOUT THE BOOK

I want to share what inspired me to write this book. Although the title of the book may seem too philosophical, trust me, it is not. I will break down the title. This will help you understand why readers should pick up this book. And, if it is worth their time, money, and emotions. (First the title of this book was " life, karma and human stories" later I changed it to "THE RIPPLE EFFECT") But the intention behind writing the book remains the same.

LIFE: I am not a life coach, motivational speaker, or self-help guru (I have nothing against them). I am not claiming that this book will change your life. If it does, that's the grace of the divine. In this book, I refer to life and look at it from a middle-class man's point of view. We, kids born in the 80s, had the best childhood, they say, and I agree. Back then, life was different. Every household had almost the same struggles. No father had to bear the mountains of EMIs, and no mothers had to fight depression. Grandmothers were always ready to tell stories. Load shedding was the best thing that could happen. studies were not a burden on children, no performance pressure was put on children to be all rounder in every field. As soon as the currents went off in summer It brought all the friends in the colony to the adda. There, they shared stories from their elders or from here and there. Nobody could say the other was lying as there was no Google to find the truth. Such stories make a special room in our hearts forever. We may forget the friend's name but not the story. (As a teacher and a child psychologist, I ask the education department to add storytelling to the curriculum.)

So, as I talk about life, we all enjoyed that in life by listening to short stories, but our children didn't. So, it occurred to me, why not pass it on. Imagine four female friends walking home from the bus stop to their houses in this series. what they must be chatting about, telling stories about, discusssing some serious topics such as karma and all, maybe some of us did so when we were young. We were so consumed with emotions and stories, sometimes suspense, sometimes horror, sometimes lighter that we shared among friends while walking on the road that we wished that road would never end and we never reached home till the story ended. In short, I am trying to relive and recreate the 1990s era.

The author wrote this book in that format.

KARMA: Karma is a complicated term. Many books cover the topic of karma. And, chapters in the Bhagwat Geeta explain it in detail. There are some things that we can't understand. But, should we stop studying them? For example, I am not as good at understanding math. I don't get how Albert Einstein found $e=mc^2$. But that doesn't stop me from learning 2+2=4. Right? Right. In a few of the stories, I have shed light on how our past life karmas have an effect on our current life. Karma is simple. You reap what you sow. If you forget what you've sown, surrender to the divine. He will care for you. Life is never fair or unfair; it's always between. We choose each moment; we smile and surrender, or we curse and surrender. Intending to smile or curse creates karma. Because, in the end, you MUST surrender. This is my simple understanding of 2+2.

HUMAN STORIES: This book contains human stories. They are all based on real events and the stories that I have heard growing up. Most of them are from my own life. I only changed the names. Each day we add a stitch to the fabric of life. Sometimes, the stitch is smooth, but sometimes the thread gets knotted. The knot can be so ugly(here I mean by creating conflicts with people in our lives) at times that we forget that we can buy a new thread and start over instead of untangling the knot and starting stitching again. More complex are human stories, much more than life and karma. God gave life. He said to watch your karma. We humans are ungrateful. We waste life grumbling. We forget that we are here to learn.

Love and Light,

Deepa

CONTENTS

AMMAN

Namaskar, welcome to the Karkhanis family in Konkan. (Konkan is the coastal stretch of Maharashtra). The outstanding quality of the Konkani people is that they are very hard-working and extremely honest. Their honesty and loyalty are unmatched. Not only do the people of Konkan make this place beautiful, but nature has also graced this place with beautiful beaches, cashew nut trees, coconut trees, and its awesome cuisine.

Now about the Karkhanis family: the era from which I am narrating this story is around the 1960s. Karkhanis were zamindars, a joint and wealthy family. The family consists of Vishwambhar Karkhanis, who was the sarphanch (head) of the village"Panjurle.". Vishwambhar's wife was" Shakuntala Kharkhanis.". They had a daughter, "Jijai Karkhanis," who was just like a doll. She was a young little girl who always wore a parker polka (skirt top) with two pleats, was center-parted, was very fair, and she loved wearing small green and red bangles.

Whenever Vishwanbhar would get ready and start wearing his kolhapuri chappals, Jijai would go running towards him and say, "Baba, if you are going to town today, please get me new ribbons or get me new bangles; these have become old now, and moreover, I am bored of wearing them. But don't worry, I will pass them on to Jai." Jai was Jijai's cousin, the daughter of Ashok and Savitri Karkhanis. Vishwambhar's mother was also alive; her name was Kamala Bai Karkhanis. His father was the Sarpanch too when he was alive. Villagers respected Vishambhar's father as an authoritative figure in the village. For any land settlements or petty household quarrels, his verdict was final. Nobody dared to go against it. Karkhanis owned most of the land in the village and did farming of cashew nuts, coconuts, jackfruits, and high-grade Alphonso mangoes. They were the wealthiest family in the village, and they provided labour to many families.

Houses in Konkan are called "wada'," so this house was known as "Karkhanisanncha wada," which means karkhanis mansion. The wada was a huge square structure where the centre of the house was kept 'open to the sky, known as "Bhramasthan," and the rooms surrounded the four sides. The washroom was outside the house, and there was a swing where Vishwambhar used to swing when people came to meet him. People were not allowed to climb the stairs; they had to sit down and talk about whatever they had to ask or tell. Nobody dared to lift their heads up. This rule applied even to his brother Ashok. Why? Because he had committed one mistake of cheating his elder brother in money matters, it had gone on for quite a long time until one day, when Vishwambhar caught him red-handed, putting farmers' earned money into his own pocket. That act of Ashok would have brought shame to the Karkhanis family if it went unnoticed, Vishwambhar felt. He had asked Ashok to leave the house, but Kamala Bai meddled and solved the matter. From that day on, both brothers didn't speak much to each other.

But it is different with their wives and their daughters. Shakuntala and Savitri were like sisters to each other. The relationship between their husbands did not influence their relationship. Most of the time they would be in the kitchen, grinding, cooking, sweeping the big verandah, pulling water from the well, and doing the work. There were no tiles, so they had to even carpet it with dung. This kept them busy, and they also had their mother-in-law to look after. Kamala Bai was very happy with both of her daughter-in-laws.

Sisters Jijai and Jai also shared a very special bond; they were inseparable. Both loved each other immensely. Their grandmother sat in the front yard, and these two angels played "ghar ghar" there. They would get small utensils from the kitchen, keep three stones, put some sticks inside and act like lighting a fire, cook stuff on that, and later give it to their grandmother to eat. Then Granny had to decide whose dish was better.

Jai's or Jijai's?. She always avoided answering, and she hugged both of them. But today both did not listen to Granny; they wanted the answer.

Jijai said, "Ajji, you always do this; you have to tell me today."

Jai said, "Ajji, not only do you have to decide, but you will also have to award the best dish today."

Kamala Bai smiled and said, "Ok, ok, go bring your dishes first; they were covered. Ajji said, Jai, keep your plate in my right hand, and Jijai, keep yours in my left hand, and turn your backs and stand. I will taste it and announce the winner.

As soon as Kamala Bai opened the lid, she started laughing because she found that both her granddaughters had put 2 pinches of sugar on the plate and asked her who was the best chef. Ajji's laughter turned into a smile when both her granddaughters asked her, " Ajji sang na?" meaning Granny tell, Na. Kamala Bai called them both near, hugged them both, and said, You know what? In this year's mandirs yatra, I will buy you both a new Parker polka. Both Jai and Jijai started dancing in joy.

Panjurale village had a very ancient temple of a devi. All the residents called her Amma and believed that Amma never brought any draught or feminine to the crops; she was their protector. She was a fierce form of a Female deity. Every year, there used to be a sacrificial festival where hens were sacrificed.

There was a legend that the demons that the Amma Goddess captured had to be fed blood at least once a year, and the Amma Goddess would be happy with a simple payasam. This is one of the biggest occasions Panjurale looks forward to every year. Guests are called from all around the place. Neighbouring village people come with their pleas to Amma. Stalls are set up, lights are put up everywhere, dishes are cooked in every house, children are happy, and women of the houses are busy preparing delicacies for the guests, but the most important part of the function is not all this but a goosebump moment during the arti time when the goddess Amma herself comes into the body of the priest and tells whatever she has to tell to the people of the village, her own children. She warns them if they are going wrong or what needs to be done to keep the place in peace and prosperity. This process takes hardly a minute or two, but whoever sees it is considered to be blessed forever.

Vishwambhar's father, as I said, was a respectable man and had the honour of Arti till he was alive; nobody else could take that honour away from him. After his father's death, the question was where to find such an honest and true man. because Amma puja cannot be performed by anyone with a greedy heart. One night after Sr. Kharkhanis death, the Amma Goddess came in the dream of the priest and said that from this year on, Vishwambhar Karkhanis will continue doing my puja; you people will not have to search for anyone outside. I am going to bless the couple with a daughter, just like a "nakshatra" (star), which he has been longing for but has never asked for or prayed even in silence.

Vishwambhar and Shakuntala were blessed with a daughter; they named her Jijiai. She was Amma's blessing.

After a year, Ashok (his younger brother) and Savitri were also blessed with a daughter, Jai.

As in the olden days, sharing things and passing on elder sibling's clothes to younger ones was natural; jijai's clothes and other things like bangles and anklets, whichever did not fit her, were given to Jai. There were no ill feelings in anybody's mind. Jai, too, liked it. Jijai loved Jai. Jijai was too talkative, and Jai was an introvert. Jai listened to all that Jijai had to say. Jijai knew how to ask for things and how to get things done, like asking her Baba to get new ribbons or new bangles anyway; she was the nakshatra, as the goddess Amma had said, but that doesn't mean Jai was a neglected child; even though she was equally loved and cared for, as she was sort of an introvert, she expressed herself less and did not like others to express to much love towards her.

The month of Chaitra (roughly summer, after Holi) was nearing, and everywhere the preparations for the mandir's annual function had started. Jai and Jijai had not forgotten the reward. They were behind their ajji for their parkar polka. Finally, Ajji gave in, and when Vishwanbhar was going to Karwar city, Ajji handed him some money and said, Vishwa, see, the temple festival is coming, and I have promised these girls that I will make them new dresses. Please would you buy a few metres of cloth, enough for both the girls, and matching bangles? Vishwa smiled and nodded yes.

The whole day, both sisters were waiting patiently for Baba to return with the new dress and matching bangles. Baba came back in the evening, and both girls came running out of the house, snatching the cloth bag from his hand, and went running to Ajji Ajji Ajji to see what Baba had bought. Kamala Bai opened the bag and found two pieces of khun cloth (khun is a special type of material that is the specialty of karnataka and Maharashtra), but there were two different colors: green and deep brown. Kamala Bai came out of the room and asked Vishwa, Why did you buy two different colours? He said AAI did not find the same colors; I was in a hurry, so I had to buy two different colors. Please adjust this time.

Kamala Bai went inside and told her granddaughters that tomorrow we will give these to stitch to the neighbour Nayak's house and tell her to give them by Thursday night so that you can try them on Friday. Friday is the auspicious day to try on new clothes; today is Monday, so there are enough days for her to finish your dresses.

The girls were just counting the days and sitting and chatting about which ribbons would look good and which bangles would look good. Those were the days when people used to buy dresses only once a year and would literally put haldi kumkum on them before wearing them because it was considered a form of Laxmi.

Thursday arrived, and from morning till noon 4 times, Jijai asked Ajji,When shall we go to Nayak Kakus house to get our dresses? Ajji couldn't stop them; she said to go and check when she would give and tell Kaku, I will pay her later. Both started running; Ajji also remembered something and came running to the door and said, Jai, Jija, go slowly. The wall of the well is broken in Nayak's house. Go slowly, ha ha ajji. After 10 minutes, they came home with long faces,Kaku said in the evening. Ajji said it was ok; we will get it tomorrow, ok? Both said okay and went out to play.

At sunset, Jai and Jijai were playing in the backyard, and suddenly Jijai whispered in Jai's ear, Come, let's go to Nayak Kakus's house and get our dresses. Let us not tell Ajji and Aai, or else they will scold us. We will go immediately and come back. Jai was a bit reluctant, but she somehow agreed. In excitement, both went running through the back door in the narrow lane with no street lights, then took a turn to Nayak's house. As they were running in darkness, Jai tripped on the rock and fell in well. Jijai, unaware of this as she was ahead, went inside and asked Nayak kaKu, "Are the dresses ready?"? Kaku was surprised to see Jijai alone so late in the evening. She asked, "Have you come alone?" Jijai said, "No, Jai is also with me; she was just behind me.".

Nayak Kaku smelled something fishy and came out running, peeped into the broken well, and saw ripples of water. She understood and screamed her lungs out. Jijai was not in a position to understand anything.

Suddenly there was mourning in the village atmosphere. The temple ceremony was near, and it had to be done, but the Karkhanis had lost their little daughter Jai. They had no choice but to attend the arti as it was their honor. With tears in their eyes and questions in their hearts, all the members of the family asked the same question: Why, Amma, why, why? Why, Jai, what paap (bad deeds) had she done at such a young age? But Amma also chooses to remain silent.

According to Hindu tradition, nobody is supposed to wear new clothes on occasion, nor are they allowed to celebrate any festivals or auspicious events when there is a death in the family. It is their mourning period. Usually, all the big festivals are not celebrated for a year.

Days passed by, and Jijai was missing her best friend, Jai. Jijai had started becoming more silent. It had been almost a year since Jai's death, and things in the house had started coming back to normal except for Jijai, who used to talk a lot earlier and now had chosen silence as her way of life.

In June, it was Jijai's birthday, and her mother asked Jijai to wear her new dress, the one she had gotten stitched for the yatra, put mala in her hair, put on new bangles, and then accompany her to Amma Temple.

Jijai just smiled, nodded, and said she would be ready. Her mother next morning looked at her daughter, who actually looked like a goddess to her and said, "Konachi nazar na logo," 'Keep away from the evil eye." Her mother held the pooja thali in hand, and from the back gate, both of them started walking towards the mandir. As they were crossing the Nayaks well, Jijai turned her neck, and the whole incident flashed in front of her eyes. She heard someone calling her "Jija.".

She looked at her mom. They went to the mandir, had darshan, and came home. As soon as Jijai came home, she started feeling cold and had a high fever. She had stopped eating anything; two days passed, and home remedies did not work, so finally, the village Vaidya was called home. He checked her nadi and said there was nothing to worry about. maybe her periods are on the way and it happens to some, so don't take tension After a week, everything came back to normal, and she started feeling well.

Last year, due to Jaii's death,they did not celebrate any festivals. The women of the house thought maybe Diwali would cheer Jijai. Diwali Padwa is an auspicious day. Everyone wears new clothes and gets ready,and the elders bless the younger ones. Savitri, Jai's mother, came to Jijai and said," Darling, I have lost my daughter, you are only my daughter now. What will I do to keep her new unused dress bangles and anklets with me? Please, can you wear it for me on Padwa Day? I feel Jai has come back. I miss her a lot, Jija. I miss her a lot.". She hugged Jijai and cried. Both cried till their hearts melted.

The sun appeared more graceful on Padwa day. All the wada was decorated with orange and yellow marigold flowers and mango and Ashoka leaves. The wada was looking majestic, like it'd been standing there for so many years. The women in the house were up before sunrise, and the rangolis were drawn everywhere. Men were in their dhotis coats and fetas, women in their fine naraynpeth and nath; it was a scene to watch, JiJai came out wearing jais green colour Khun parker polka with red bangles red ribbons, black kajal and brown bindi She bowed down and touched everyone's feet in the house. As she was stepping inside the threshold of the house after watering the tulsi plant, she heard someone call her name from behind. Jija, she thought, must have missed hearing it before she stepped her right foot inside the house. The voice calling her name became more clear and angrier... Jija turned back and saw no one. She got scared but had no guts to tell anyone.

Now this started happening regularly whenever she stepped out; she heard a voice calling her in anger. Jijai started becoming more and more silent; she hardly spoke to anyone so to cheer her up, her ajji Kamala Bai used to make her sleep on her lap and tell stories, and her Baba used to get her colourful bangles and ribbons, but whenever she wore them, the voice that called her name became angrier and angrier. Now JiJai started feeling that someone's shadow was constantly watching her. Jijai felt she was never alone; she could not tell anyone, as she thought her family would think she had lost her mind.

Within a few days, Jijai started falling sick again, with a cold and fever. Aging Vaidya was called, and he gave some kadha (herbal medicine), but nothing seemed to work. The situation was getting worse; she had stopped taking food. The women of the house were fasting for her recovery. Vishwambhar had taken a vow that he would bring Jijai to Ganpati Pule to Bappa's darshan; once she becomes well (Ganpati Pule is the western sentinel god of India; it is a swayanbhu Ganpati temple), it is still believed that whatever wishes you ask Ganpati here are surely fulfilled.

Jijai started becoming pale; she had lost tremendous weight, and only the skeleton was visible; her hair was falling off; her nails were falling off; and her beautiful skin already had wrinkles. This was happening to a 14-year-old girl. It was worse than death for her. Nobody understood the way out. All the relatives were flocking in all day and night, and whoever told them any remedy, both their mother and aunt were immediately ready to do it. They had lost one nakshatra (Jai); they did not want to lose the other.

Chaitra was near; the annual yatra had to be carried out; no excuses could be given. Preparations were over, and finally, the day of asthami had arrived when the Karkhanis family had to perform the honouring arti. Vishwambhar was reluctant to take Jijai to the temple because he thought people would enjoy the drama unnecessarily. But Kamala Bai said to let Amma's dristi fall on her, and Vishwambhar agreed.

Ammas Murti was made up of black stone, and she sat with folded legs in padmasana. Her one hand is a trident, and the other is carrying a chakra; her front hand is an abhaya mudra, and the other is carrying a sword. She is wearing a beautiful red sari with green borders, and she is fully decorated with jasmine flowers. There are no artificial lights in the temple, only tall oil lamps, and that makes Amma Devi look so divine and mesmerising that tears start flowing down their eyes for no reason. Jijai was made to sleep in the sanctum sanatorium, and the arti started with loud dhol, bells, and loud music.

Vishwanbhar was rotating the arti and tears were flowing down his eyes. Arti was about to get over. Everyone was chanting *Hare Rama Hare Rama Ram Ram Hare Hare Hare Krishna Hare Krishna Krishna Krishna Hare Hare.*

After arti priests come in a particular attire, they follow certain rituals and deities and are usually like the messengers of the god to the normal people. These priests tell us how the rains will be for the year and which crops will do well. There are few good things about living a happy life, but these days, such things are vanishing. So, Vishwambhar Karkhanis and his family were sitting around where the priests were performing a dance, usually, so the priest started by praising the lord and inviting all the gods from heaven to join this function. For the first few minutes, he spoke about the rains and the crops, then he came near Jijai, looked deep into her eyes, and laughed loudly.

He asked Vishwanbhar, "You have two daughters? Hahaha. You have two."

Vishwanbhar was confused. The priest said, "Do you know where the second daughter of your family is?"

Vishwanbhar said, "Yes, she left us a few years ago."

The priest laughed again. "Hahahahahah."

The laugh was so loud and scary that people witnessing it had chills on their spines.

The priest said, "No, she has never left anywhere; see, look at this child carefully; your daughters are here only."

Half the people who were listening to this Karkhanis family were in shock; they did not understand what the priest meant.

The priest asked, "Does your daughter fall ill when she wears something new?"

Kamala Bai answered; we never noticed

The priest asked, "Has your daughter been wearing something that belonged to the dead one?"

Suddenly Savitri remembered, "She said, Guruji, I had asked Jijai to wear his dress, bangles, and anklets.

jija gave back the bangles and the dress, but I guess she is still wearing Jai anklets. Oh, deva, Savitri said,and she collapsed.

Then the priest came forward, removed the anklets from the Jijais ankles, and kept them aside. He sat crossed-legged in front of them and explained, "Lord Yajaman, the girl who died was a young girl, a girl full of dreams; she was on her way to get her new dress. When she fell into the well, she was not ready for the sudden death;her soul was upset and angry. Then, when she saw Jijai on her birthday, she tried to call her, but they could not connect. How could they? The soul was beyond understanding this simple logic. Next, when she saw Jija wearing her new dress, she got really furious. She thought, "How dare she use my things?"?

As Jija did not remove Jai's anklets and give them back, she got more and more jealous and started following her everywhere. This made Jija sick, as she was surviving on her energy Everyone was in tears

Kamala Bai asked the priest, "Yajaman, please tell me what can be done to get rid of all this now."

The priest said, "The soul is attached to the stuff; please offer all the things that you give to a newlywed bride and pray to jai's soul not to trouble Jijai; she is your sister. Also, some havan and shanti need to be done so that the lost soul finds its way to go towards light. jai's soul is failing to accept that it is dead and it cannot have all this stuff, it is lost.

We smother our secret fears of impermanence by surrounding ourselves with more than more goods, more and more things and more comforts, only to find ourselves their slaves.

The Tibetan Book of Living and Dying

A psychic attack is a deliberate and malicious energy attack from either a dark entity or a spirit entity. This can manifest suddenly as feeling stressed out for no reason, feeling anxious and weird, unexplained body pain, feelings of exhaustion, extensive negative thinking, exaggerated fears and even questioning your own sanity. It is not uncommon when a dark entity attacks in this way they knock us off down, and we are often not in the space or frame of mind we need to be in to clear them

PAKHIMAA

Realise that everything connects us to everything else.
Leonardo da Vinci

"This jaibird eagerly waits for sunrise every night, when he goes to sleep."

Location: West Bengal's East Midnapore District.

"Chandan, wake up; it's already late," yelled Chandan's maa. Your father has already reached the farms. Hurry up, boy. Do you want an earful today too?

But, maa, you know, I don't like to work in farms, argues a 14-year-old Chandan Chanda.

"Look, Chandan, food doesn't come served and decorated on our plates daily. If you don't help your Baba in farming, where do you think food will come from?

These voices were coming from a small hut. Sheela, Chandan's sister, was washing vessels outside the hut, and she was thinking to herself, Every morning, the same dialogues between dada and maa. When will this change? Dada doesn't like farming, Maa never leaves his back, and Baba is always agitated. "Hey Maa," are you even listening to our prayers? Each day, it's becoming more difficult to catch up with this poverty.

Chandan left with no choice and ran without chappals towards the paddy farms to help his baba. Why without slippers? They couldn't afford it, and when we don't get what we desire, we usually learn to adapt to live with it or without it. Circumstance is a great teacher because it doesn't give you a chance to complain about it. Keeping sane with a teenage boy is not so easy for his Baba. Both just tolerated each other. The reason is that we, as humans, have lost many virtues in the name of modernity. We are trying to keep up our steps with time, whereas we forget that time cannot come into anyone's hand, not even Lord Rama's or Lord Krishna's. One such virtue that we lost along the way is the art of listening to others. We do not have the patience or empathy to understand what the other person wants to say. We, as humans, instead of learning new things, should try to unlearn what we have learned over the years.

So the main problem between Chandan and his Baba was that his Baba never wanted to hear what Chandan was really interested in doing. Chandan was a school dropout, and economic conditions were getting worse, so it was taken for granted by Chandan's parents that he should do farming like his Baba. But Chandan had other dreams; he always wanted to be an artist. He loved drawing, painting, and acting, but to his parents, these were rich people's pleasures, not money-making crafts.

Chandan had a passion for painting since he was a little boy. Although he started to paint, lack of money and no family support kept him from continuing. He couldn't tell his parents about his bent towards art because, firstly, he was very introverted by nature, and secondly, he surely knew they would neither like this as a profession nor support him. Finally, he made up his mind and chose art over farming to pursue his artistic career.

On a misty winter night, he boarded a train towards Kolkata, the city of his dreams.

Till here, Chandan's life was a struggle—not even an average life—being brought up in poverty, then leaving behind his family and finding a workplace in such a big city seems sorrowful. But from this point on, the story takes a different turn. Let's see how MAYA (illusion) and KARMA play hide and seek with Chandan. Not only that, but this true story of Chandan Chanda compelled us to question whether boons and curses are as real as they seem. or whether they too are part of this grand illusion called MAYA?

Chandan knew no one in Kolkata; actually, this would be wrong to say in this manner because our cosmic mother MAA **(Goddess)** Kali resides there, and Chandan also decided to be dependent on Goddess for his survival. He used to go and sit in the mandir (temple) of Dakshineswar daily, praying for some miracle to happen in his life, as he had started questioning his decision. But MAA is MAA; her heart goes out to every child, rich or poor; all are hers. In the temple, he came across a Dutta family, who, by the grace of Goddess Kali, had sympathy for him and gave Chandan a place to stay. This young boy did whatever petty chores he was told to do and also found a shelter. Basic needs were taken care of, and now he had to concentrate on the dream for which he had come to Kolkata. He started meeting people in search of learning the art,and like an angel, a professor from Rabindra Bharati University drove him to Kumartuli, the epicenter of clay idol production. He picked up the skill of creating clay idols here and learned to master the skill here before returning to his hometown of Midnapore.

Idol-making is a skill very few can master; Chandan has mastered that. But clay idols are in demand only around Durga Puja. The rest of the year, he had to sit ideally, so he learned photography and fine arts. In the months when he was not making idols, he went out doing photography. He was also interested in drama. He taught drama to kids in his free time. Years went by, and the poor chap had accomplished his dream. Meanwhile, he lost his father, who accepted his art and agreed that they were wrong and that he could make money from art. Chandan got married and was living a happy, fulfilling life until one unfortunate night, when life took the worst turn for Chandan.

Mother Earth is like a school for all of us souls; we come here to learn lessons, to experience emotions, and to spread love and peace. Every soul, depending on its *prarabdha,* must learn certain lessons. Before we take birth, when we are in higher realms, we decide to come down upon earth to learn particular unlearned lessons, and so we **choose** the circumstances accordingly. But after birth, we forget all these processes because the cosmic illusion takes over. The play of cosmic intelligence is so grand that the situations in one's life are planned to the finest detail. And the timing of this cosmic intelligence can never go wrong.

We, as humans, break down life into bits and pieces; we divide it into hours, days, and years, but the cosmos has been carrying out *karmic* accounts from time infinite, and here time is not linear. As soon as intelligence feels it's time for karma's fruit to ripen, it will just push it down into your life. whether you are ready for it or not, your choice is not taken into consideration. You may be a very good person, but that doesn't prevent bad things from happening to you. You blame God, destiny, or whatever; it's of no use, because you will have to bear the consequences of that bad effect. You don't even remember when you committed that karma, but *karma* serves fruit at the right time, whether you like it or not.

One night of the year 2004 altered the entire outlook of Chandan's life. A horrible incident takes place, and a free bird named Chandan is kept captive forever. now a lifer, convicted for a crime. He is serving a life sentence at Midnapore Central Correctional Home.

So, what happened that night?

A group of children had gathered at Chandan's house to rehearse the skit that they were going to perform. Chandan was the mentor, so he supervised the act. The kids gathered for rehearsal. That evening, Chandan had some urgent work, so he told the children to go ahead with the practice, which he was doing only out of love for art. His wife was washing dishes outside the house. She suddenly heard a loud noise from inside where boys were practicing, and she was awestruck at what she saw. A terrible incident occurred while one child was portraying Khudiram, the freedom fighter from Bengal. The kid, who playfully wrapped the rope around his neck as they practiced the scene where Khudiram would be hanged, accidentally noosed himself out and died as he was in midair hanging himself. Neither Chandan nor his wife were present on the spot. These boys believed Shaktiman (a popular TV show for children) would come to save him, so they started shouting Shaktiman's name, but in vain. Seeing that, they got frightened and ran away.

The parents of the deceased kid accused Chandan of murdering their son. Due to a paucity of evidence and Chandan's inability to establish his innocence, Chandan was declared guilty. He has been imprisoned for life. Serving a murder sentence at Midnapore Central Correctional Home since 2004.

Well, if we look back at Chandan's life, we can see how destiny conspired all throughout his life, being born into a poor family, and instead of choosing farming like his father, why did he like art? Why did he choose Kolkata only to run? He was an art teacher; he could have set the play on any national hero. Why the "*Fansi* of Khudiram"? Can we see a pattern here?

Chandan's main *karma* to fulfil in this lifetime was to serve life in Jai. But his soul was a good one; he wouldn't have killed anyone by his own hands and then gone to Jail. Being a silent and introverted character, he was interested only in his work, with no hustle or tussle with other people. He is a calm and composed-minded person, so how can he serve a life sentence in Jail for such behaviour?

So now the secondary *karma,* or his *samskaras,* came into play. *Samskaras* are the impressions we carry from many lifetimes. For example, if we see a 4-year-old kid playing a musical instrument with great accuracy, do you think she learned it in her lifetime? No, not for sure; she must have been an *ustad* in some of her previous lifetimes. These samskaras usually don't leave us easily. In the same way, in Chandan's case, his samskaras of being good at art pulled him to fulfil his destiny of spending his entire lifetime in prison. Cosmos, or higher intelligence, or God, whatever you call it, has its own way of pulling you to learn your lessons; you can't escape that.

Chandan accepted fate and behaved well while imprisoned. Later, Chandan was sent to an open prison because of his good behaviour. He is allowed 12 hours every day to go out of prison to work. He leaves the Jai grounds at six in the morning, and by sunset, he must return and spend the night in Jail. Years have gone by, and Chandan is doing this. He paints the walls of the city with his beautiful graffiti. Also, he makes Durga idols in Jail; not only that, but he also teaches his art to his jail inmates, who may go out and start their own work.

Many politicians visit the jail to see how reformed the prisoners are. One such incident was when Chandan went to New Delhi to meet former president Pratibha Devi Singh Patil. Chandan gifted her a clay idol made by his hands and named it "Pakhimaa.". (Meaning a Mother (in the form of a bird) looking at her children with compassion.) Through this, Chandan wanted to convey the message to the President of India: Please be my mother and release me from this cage forever But that went unnoticed, and Chandan was not heartbroken by it. When I had a conversation with him, he said, "You know, Didi, sometimes I feel it is a boon that I am in Jail; so many great personalities come to meet me here; I get to do my art; I complete my idols; if I were outside, hardly anyone would know me.".

This is the simplicity of Chandan, and so I am sure that even God could not be cruel to him. God gave him name and fame; it's his outlook, and Chandan takes it very positively. Does he deserve this? We are nobody to answer that. We don't even have the right to answer it.

When I asked him, does this injustice make you angry? How do you feel about the people who put you behind bars?

Chandan says, "Didi I don't think much about that, you know why, because here I get to do what I love the most, and about the people who put me behind bars, even if they have lost something precious. I have no sick feelings for them.

As I said earlier, one man's boon can be a curse to another man. Just like the boon of having a child by chanting a *mantra,* which Kunti got and tried out of excitement, was a boon to her, but all throughout her life, that curse followed Karna like a shadow, giving him only insults and humiliation. But Chandan, just like Karna, made use of that curse and turned it into a boon for themselves. There are extraordinary people among us who are the wisest teachers because they walk the path; they don't preach.

CHANDAN EXTENSION

After reading Chandan's story, we really feel sorry for whatever he has gone through in life. Not only for Chandan, but most of the time we feel sorry for ourselves. We ask God, Why has this suffering come my way? Why me? Those who do bad are happy, but those who do good suffer all their lives. Is this true? Do you believe that any human is free of pain or suffering? No human is free of pain or suffering. It is up to us if we want to keep that pain as pain or convert it into suffering. How? I will tell you.

My grandmother is about 78 years old now. By God's grace, she is not bedridden or anything. She is independent. She does everything on her own. She is diabetic and cannot hear from one ear; apart from that, I can say she is healthy for her age. Now I want to explain how pain and suffering are different. In 2001, I lost my grandfather. My grandmother lost her best friend and life partner; they were married at the youthful age of 12 years (in those days, child marriage was not illegal). Then in 2017, she lost her younger sister; in 2018, she lost her daughter (my mom) after 3 months of my mother's death;, she lost my uncle (mama) in 2020; she lost her son-in-law (my father); and in 2020, she lost her other son (my elder mama). Since January 2018, she has seen the deaths of her son and daughter. Imagine the immense pain she must have gone through seeing their dead bodies. From cradle to grave. She saw the whole cycle. No parent would ever like to even think of this in their mind, but she faced it three times. That is pain.

But she accepted the truth and the reality. She knew nothing else could be done about this. Acceptance is liberating. And that helped her endure the pain. She did not magnify it in her mind, never felt she was the victim, held the thought of the victim mentality, and made it into suffering for herself. If it were someone else in her place, I am sure they would have slipped into depression. But she did not, just because she never thought she was the victim and God was unfair to her. She just accepted what came into her life, and she is still alive, living each day at a time.

As I said, no human is free of pain and suffering anywhere in the world. Imagine the scene where we would see on the highway all the cars bumping into each other as they all want to speed, and no one can stop. Pain is the brake on our lives. We may not like it, but like bitter medicine, it is necessary. God made humans by putting a lot of thought into them.

He also came down in the human form of LORD RAM and LORD KRISHNA to set an example of how even God in human form cannot escape from the pain, but they can choose not to suffer and keep the smile intact.

Acceptance is liberating.

BETWEEN RAILWAY LINES

I am sure many of us love trains, travelling by trains, or just watching them pass by. The noise and the speed of it are so magnetic. I remember when we were small, we used to wave at the passengers from the gate and jump with happiness when they waved back.

Little Gyan: Bori Bunder, located in Mumbai, was the first railway station in India. India's first passenger train ran from Bori Bunder to Thane in 1853. Wait wait! Why am I telling you so much about trains? Because the lovers of the story are in love because of the train.

This story is set in the 1950's. Revati Guha was the only child of Satyavati Guha and Mahendra Singh Guha. Revati, or Rati, was an exceptionally beautiful Bengali girl. Her father, Mahendra Singh, had transferred from north India to Mumbai in the railway department. Revati's mother was a calm lady. Both loved Revati very much. Revati missed Bengal. She had her grandparents there, as well as her cousins; she missed eating fish too. She was almost sixteen, completed her 10th grade, and was helping her mother with the household work, which was not so hectic as Mahendra Singh was at a good post in the railway department, so they had servants full time. Revati loved trains, she used to ask her dad to take her along with him.

She was so charming that whoever she smiled at, would have never forgotten her face.

Mahindra Babu used to take her along some days when she complained she was bored and wanted to go back to Kolkata.

As soon as she entered Mahendra Babus's office, she would sit on his chair and stare out of the window. The trains passed from there. She loved to watch them pass. She loved to listen to their sound. She sat there as if she were in a trance. That place gave her some sort of solace. Her trance was disturbed by the knock on the door. "Mahendra Babu," someone inquired, "se niscaya ekhane kotha ache" (he must be somewhere here), Revati said hurriedly, looking at a tall, handsome boy. Oh, baba nahi, she showed him with a gesture. And she went running out of the office, hiding her face with her yellow sari. "Thika ache sona" amara nama Abhay bagechi hataa'ana banghaliun" Listen, my name is Abhay Bagchi,even though I am Bengali.

That day, Revati went home, hugged her mom, and told her, Mani, maybe I am not missing Kolkata that much.

Her mom smiled at her and said she was happy that Revati realised that change in life is permanent.

The next day, again, Revati went to her baba's office, but this time she was not waiting for the train but for that Bengali, whose eyes she had prepared to look deep into. She knew the time when her baba went for the inspection, and so did this new joinee, Abhay Bagchi. Abhay used to come to give the half-day report before lunchtime, but after two days, he started finding a godly-looking beauty on his sir's chair.

Abhay Bagchi came from a poor family. His dad was not so educated, and his mom, Anusaya, was the actual head of the family. She was the one who made all the decisions for everyone. Nobody spoke a word beyond Anusaya.

Abhay's childhood was not as playful or colourful as Revati's. Revati's parents were understanding and free-minded. made her grow up into an independent woman. In the 1950, when women's education was not a big deal, she had completed her matriculation. For Abhay, it was all the opposite; his father, Andhaka, had totally surrendered to his mom, Anusaya.

Anasuya was the boss because she thought she kept the house in order, as did her son. But love understands no orders, no boundaries, and no distances. This train station had slowly become the nest of these new lovebirds. They hardly spoke. He asked her name, and she said Revati, she would sit on a chair, and he would sit near the window, and both watched the passing train. She sometimes bought Sandesh for him and gave it to him when her baba was away, and he bought her raw tamarinds, which she cherished. He also collected the jasmine flowers for her because she had long, flowing hair. She used to string them in front of him while watching the train pass by, and she wore them just while stepping out of the office so that Abhay could smell them.

Abhay had found everything in Revati: a childish girl, a mature friend, an understanding partner, and a soulmate for life. Abhay did not want to waste time. He went to Anusaya and Andhaka and confessed his love for Revati. First, Anusaya was furious. "How would you bypass me to take such a major decision?" But later, she calmed down.

Anusaya was happy from the inside but did not express it.

When Abhay approached Revati's parents with the proposal, Mahendra Babu was at a fix because he knew Abhay and his work; he was a sincere and hardworking man, but he was not very sure about his family.

He looked at his daughter; she was staring at the ground with no words coming out of her mouth. Then Mahendra Babu thought to himself that the only issue is that Abhay is not rich; if my daughter cannot adjust there, surely I can make different arrangements for the whole family, and my samskaras that I have given to her are not so weak. I am sure she will adjust; it is for her love and for her happiness only.

Revati and Abhay got married on an auspicious day. Abhay loved Revati like anything. He oiled her hair daily; he served her hot tea; and they both said something to each other and giggled. Abhay was having a dream life. "But when you are unaware, that is when the demon arrives." These were all things that started annoying Anusaya; she felt that her son had slipped from her hand.

During this, Revati gave the good news that she was pregnant; apart from Abhay and Revati, nobody was happy. Revati's condition was such that she could not go and complain to her parents. He thought this was temporary and that one day it would be fine.

After a few days, daily fights started taking place in the house. Revati could not say anything because she did not know how to give back answers;she had never done it to her parents. But she at least expected that Abhay would make his mother understand. She could not make a noise, what was her mistake? This went on for a few months, the baby was growing inside Revati's womb, and she cried for hours.

After a few days, Revati even stopped expecting any retaliation towards his mother from Abhay. She started growing increasingly silent and also stopped speaking to anyone. Even when her parents visited, she never complained or showed that she was in any kind of trouble. The day had come when Revati delivered a baby boy. That made her smile after many months. She wanted him to be a warrior, so she named him Parth. Her

Parth, Parth who will stand up for her, Parth who will fight for her, Parth who will not bring tears to his mother's eyes.Parth, who will hold her hand till the end.

Revati started spending her days and nights looking after Parth. She loved him, but she was still annoyed with Abhay that he did not stand for her. He always told her to be quiet; mom is older, and just listens to what she says. Revati, being independent-minded, did not like such injustice, but for the sake of her husband, she tolerated it.

One day Parth was playing in the verandah, Abhay was sitting and reading a book, and Anusaya was sitting near Parth and telling him stories. The story goes this way, "Partho tume jani, people claim to be rich. Look at your mommy itself; they claim they have servants, lands, and properties, but can't your nana send one servant here? How much can your grandmother do? Ok, forget about him also. Partha, you are their grandson only, na? Are you or not? Anasuya screamed, or was your mother adopted? We are duped. Oh! My fate, oh! My fate Revati was in the kitchen, and as soon as she heard this, she knew exactly what to do. She knew what her calling was, and before anyone understood, she went running out of the house. After half an hour, a peon came to Abhay's house and gave him the message that Mahendra Babu had called him at the station. Abhay got ready and went to the station. Mahendra was not in the office; he was standing out at the gate., As soon as Abhay arrived, Mahendra Babu looked deep into his eyes, and a deep feeling of betrayal struck him. They walked along the station with pin-drop silence. Abhay knew something was not good; his heart was pounding with fear. He was expecting Revati to be sitting in the office crying. As soon as they reached the office, Mahendra Babu pointed down on the railway track, where Revati's body was cut into two pieces. Her head had fallen on the other side and her torso on the other.

Maybe these are Revati's last words to her son, Parth.

"I did not wish him all the best, because that would be a lie, but I did not wish him all the worst either. I simply wished him whatever it was he deserved now; whether he deserved good things was none of my business that was between him and his karma.

On Suicide

Human life is a gift. We all know that only humans can differentiate between good and bad, or, in other words, are said to be the most intelligent of all living forms. But my question is: is only intelligence enough to live a life? What about emotions? What about other feelings? Was Revati right when she decided to take that step? Was Anusaya the trigger behind all this? Was Abhay strong enough to manage and understand what was going on with Revati's emotions, and above all, what's Partho's karma in all this?

Whenever I see an injured dog or a dog that has met with an accident and is limping, searching for water in scorching heat, these are intelligent beings; at least they do not think of ending their lives, they survive through daring hardships. Committing suicide is one of the major harms that you do to your soul. After you commit suicide, your soul is not ready to suddenly leave the body, nor does it understand where to go, nor can it know where its next destination is.

To give an analogy, just think that you are living in a rented home. You one day get angry and, filled with anger, slam the door on your partner and tell her you will never return. Now you have no plans to go anywhere, and you have no stuff. When the anger calms down, your repentance will sweep in, but it's too late.

Now your soul is lost in a dark place.

KSHAMAA (FORGIVENESS)

" Khamma Ghani" Maharaj, 'padharo mhare des'. Let me introduce myself. I am the ruins of the palace in the small village near Baniraa. Maharaj, a few decades ago, I would have proudly told you the glory and heritage of the culture of Rajasthan. What it means to be "royal". it could be seen in the walk, talk, gestures, and hobbies of the kings. In this way, queens hosted the gatherings and their hospitality. Maharaj, that royalty is missing. Money can buy luxury, but not royalty. It has to be in the blood.

Sorry to bore you about this all, but I get emotional when I speak about palaces and royalty. I am destroyed now; I have nothing more than the memories left about them. Maharaj, as you know, Rajasthan is also a land of stories and magic. From here, you will hear numerous stories of haunted palaces and haunted places. Not only that, but the puppet shows are also so famous here. So I have decided to tell you a story. But this is not about some haunted palaces; it's about an ordinary old woman. Let's see what makes this story interesting.

Whenever we suffer physical or emotional trauma, it is said that a part of our soul flees the body to survive the experience. With every cut and wound, our essence and vitality grow weaker. This process is called "soul loss.".

Maharaj, there was this beautiful small village; mostly the dance community stayed here. In those days, the caste system was at its peak. Nobody ate or drank water from the houses of the lower caste. These communities usually stayed away from the village. They were called only to do menial jobs. Few of them belong to the "rudali" sect. The females from these groups were called to mourn when death took place in any zamindar or richman's house. They were the official mourners. They wore black ghagra choli, covered their faces with black dupattas, and wore a handful of bangles. Most of them usually had green-coloured tattoos on their hands and faces, very decorative designs, which made them look as if they were wearing some unique ornament. They had a belief that after a human dies, he cannot take any ornament with him to the heavens, but as tattoos are attached to the skin, he will tag along the tattoos to the heavens along with the smoke. Usually, they tattooed something that meant the world to them, like the name of their deity, the name of their husband, or the symbol that belonged to their particular sect.

Also, zamindars followed "ghunghat pratha," where the women of the house always had to be under the veil (they could never show their faces to any other male other than their husband), and they were not allowed to express their emotions in public. They could not even cry in the crowd, even if their husband died. So the Rudalis were called on their behalf to mourn and cry loudly. Of course, they took money to do this.

Maharaj This story belongs to two sects. One is Rudali, and the other belongs to the Banjara sect or Lambani sect. Even these are nomadic sects that perform dance acts on the street and earn money. They usually roam from one village to another, performing acts like balancing on the rope and dancing while keeping six or seven pots on top of each other over their heads. Now these two sects lived on the outskirts of the village. They did not get along well with each other. They usually had a fight over the water, which was almost dry. Who would pull the water first? This was an everyday affair. This brought not only disharmony but also envy between the tribes. Rudali's thought was that we stay here permanently, so the well belongs to us, and these lambanis should not touch the water. On the other hand, Lambani thought we were helping them clean the village, getting rid of the rodents, and helping them. Still, how can they be so ungrateful?

In this brawl, the innocent children and the elderly women had to suffer. The younger generation did not like the two sects mixing or having good relations with each other. Their headsman had told Kabila to stay away from the other group of people. This feeling of envy was mutual. In the daytime, when the young men and women went out to earn their daily wages, these old ladies from both sects sat under a big banyan tree chewing tobacco, chit-chatting, gossiping, cleaning vegetables, or sometimes making patchwork razai (quilts), which would earn them extra income. And children did not go to school; they played "gilli danda" the whole day. This big banyan tree was like a second house for this old lady. They had built a sitting space around it. It provided them with shade and a cool breeze.

Now the main story starts between two protagonists. Bhanu and Ila. Both are old females who sit under the banyan tree daily for gossip. One was rudali, and the other was lambani. Both had the habit of chewing tobacco and gossiping with each other in the village. Both had the habit of using abusive language while speaking. For example, they called 'baissa in front of each other but later kept names like "bagno (fool) and jhaalar (stupid). They had a love-hate relationship; they did not get along because their thoughts did not match, and they could live without each other because only these two had found a level of comfort in their friendship. They did not care what other people thought. Many times they were told not to sit together but to act as if they were going to give a damn.

They liked it or not. Ila Baisa and Bhanu Baisa had been sharing their pain, telling how Bhanu Baisa's husband cheated on her and left with her three daughters. She had married off at a young age. Only one was left. And Ila Baisa had the pain that, when her husband was alive, they had a very good life. She lived like a queen, but because of the cursed property and the fight between her family, her husband was killed. Now she says that the same curse of fighting for property has started among her sons. Ilabaisa said, “Bhanu baisa, I curse:Let all my sons die in this land fight, and finally land goes to nobody in our family.”.

Bhanubaisa was shocked to hear such harsh words from her friend's mouth. She had never seen such a ferocious avatar of her friend, Ila Baisa. That evening, she came home early and sat quietly in one corner of the house. When her daughter came, she asked, Maasa, what happened? Are you ill? She said no word; rather, Bhanubaisa was trying to remember all the previous conversations she had with Ila Baisa.

She interospected what Ila Baisa had said, and slowly the jigsaw puzzle was fitting all the pieces in their place. Today, when Bhanu heard the curse for Ila's own sons, she felt bad and upset, thinking, Who says such things to their own sons? What kind of heartless mother is she? Then she remembered Ila telling her, "When my husband died, I was not at all affected, but rather felt relieved. I had only cursed that drunkard. Why doesn't he die and never show his face back to us again?" Ila had confessed to Bhanu that not a single tear appeared in her eyes when her husband died. Rather, she said, "Mar gayo apne karma nu maut.”.

Bhanu also realised that the whole day she kept cursing those small children whose ball came and hit us accidentally: May your leg break, may your hand break. Ila was bold and outspoken. Her mouth was full of abusive words all day long. It was Bhanu who kept her a little in control. But that day, after the introspection, Bhanu came to the conclusion that she would stay away from Ila Baisa because her company was not good for her or for her family. Bhanu thought, "What if tomorrow she curses my daughter, who is carrying a baby? I will be responsible for all this. I better be far from her. Also, her daughter has been trying to conceive for so many years. I don't want to cause any trouble at home, and because of me, it would be better if I stayed far away from her. This was the final decision of Bhanu Bai."

Bhanu Baisa started avoiding Ila Baisa the next morning. Whenever Ila called her, Bhanu gave some excuse and avoided joining her in chit-chat. It went on for a few days. Ila went to Bhanu and asked her if she had some troubles at home and if she needed any help. Bhanu answered rudely to her, saying, Stay away from my house. Ila felt bad but did not take it to heart, as she felt maybe Bhanu was having some problems with her daughter's pregnancy, which she did not want to share. Ila Baisa went away and did not bother Bhanu Baisa anymore.

A few months went by, summer was about to arrive, and like every year, there was a grand Holi celebration. Celebration of colours. Celebration of forgiving the mistakes of the past, a celebration of looking towards the bright future, a celebration of bringing sweetness in relationships (as lots of sweets are prepared), a celebration of dancing as no one is watching, to be yourself at least for a day, to remove all the artificial masks that we wear for society and just be ourselves under the colour applied by our loved ones.

Usually, widows don't play Holi. It's the festival of colours. Ila Baisa thought today would be a good day to talk to Bhanu Bai again. The dinner function was arranged at night. Ilabaisa waited till Bhanu came out of her hut. Ila went running to her and said excitedly, "Baisa, come; I have been waiting for you. Let us sit in our favourite place under the tree. I want to tell you so many things. Ila said, Let us take the food and come and sit under the tree." Ila held her hand with love and was taking her towards where they were serving food. Bhanu flunked her hand in the air and said, "Leave me, Baisa; I don't want to talk to you nor keep any relationship with you." Ila was awfully hurt and asked Baisa, "What did I do? Why are you angry with me?" Bhanu refused to answer and walked away. Ilabaisa stood there like a statue, tears flowing from her eyes and her body shivering. When Bhanu turned back, she saw Ila murmuring something in her mouth. Bhanu still did not care to come back and talk to her.

A few days went by, and whenever Bhanu left the house to fetch water or for some work, she did not see Ila sitting under that big tree. Months went by, and still, Bhanu did not see Ila, nor did she dare ask anyone about her. Her daughter had delivered a baby girl, and most of her time was spent looking after the new mother and baby. But she used to wonder in her mind, Where would Ila go? No news from her? I don't even know anyone who will tell me her whereabouts.

On a new moon night, when Bhanu was washing vessels outside her house in the dark, her neighbour came running to her and said, "Maasa, maasa, thare ko khabar hai?" (Aunty, did you get the news?) Ila Maasa's body is found floating in the well. Bhanu got frightened. She did not dare to walk towards the place where the body was kept.

This incident affected Bhanu very badly. There was no way to know how her body was found in the well. Was it a suicide, or was it a murder? There was no investigation, either. Thinking about this Bhanu started gathering information from whoever she could. Some said she had been sad for the past few days. Some said it was suicide; she was tired of her life; and some said it may be murder, but Bhanu knew what could be the motive for murder. These thoughts were making Bhanu go crazy.

Months passed by, and Bhanu got her third daughter married. Now she was all alone in the house. Her day would go by doing household chores, but as the sun started setting, she used to get anxious. She had started feeling that Ila came every night to her house to take revenge because she refused to have food with her on Holi. Initially, Bhanu would stand staring at the banyan tree, thinking Ila was sitting there waiting for her. But Bhanu had no courage to approach her. Bhanu had taken it upon herself psychologically that she had killed Ila. Day by day rather than night by night, the condition started getting worse; she started seeing Ila every night after dark. She saw that Ila had followed her inside her hut too. Bhanu tried to tell this to her daughters, but nobody seemed to believe her. Ila did not hurt Bhanu at all; she would only stare at her and ask with her eyes,Why, Bhanu, what did I do to you? I had considered you my best friend. You too deserted me? ". Nothing was said in words. All the conversation was through the eyes. From one soul to another. One soul was hurt and expecting an apology, and the other soul was scared and did not understand that it needed forgiveness.

Bhanu realised that their friendship had been damaged beyond repair, and she felt a deep sense of regret for not being able to communicate with Ila properly. The silence between them spoke volumes, echoing the pain and misunderstanding that had come between them.

That night, two plates were served in the hut of Bhanu Baisa, but no food was touched. Only Bhanu Baisaa's body was found lying near the plate. It was thought to be a cardiac arrest. One friend had come to take the other friend along with her.

The tragic incident served as a stark reminder of the importance of communication and forgiveness in maintaining relationships. The bond between Bhanu and Ila was broken, but their story would live on as a cautionary tale for others.

Sometimes a simple apology can be the best medicine for the worst of the wounds. Wounds like the ego cannot be seen and cannot be measured for how deep they are. Nobody becomes smaller by saying sorry or apologizing. Being right is good, but most of the time, peace is much better. You can be right all your life, but you can't guarantee peace in every place, every relationship, and every workplace. Being humble is a virtue; not everybody has it. Let us try to develop it by surrendering to the almighty. Once we understand that we stand nowhere in front of him, we will learn to be humble. That's why the mantra " hare krishna" is " Krishna is happy even if he loses," and the winners, when they wear the winning medals, bend down low, which keeps their egos in check. In India, whenever we are honouring anyone with garland, they bend down with folded hands and accept the honor. That is humility. And a message forgives us if we have spoken or said anything inappropriate.

That is a sign of true humility and respect.

SAYONEE1: SOULMATE

"In the entire world, there is no heart for me like yours.

In the entire world, there is no love for you like mine." ~Maya Angelou

On a rainy night, at around 10 p.m., Nandini was struggling to climb the bus with a backpack on her shoulders and a trolley bag in her hand. She was heading to Bangalore, with a heavy heart and loss of words, she could only wave bye to her bestie, who had come to see her off. Nandini was frantically trying to find her seat and, for once, wanted to settle down.

She was desperately praying that the bus would start soon and hit the road. Nandini did not say goodbye to her friend nor look into her eyes, and this bus was still waiting for the passengers to fill in. She was getting restless while her friend standing near her window was giving her instructions about the city she was about to move into.

That irritated Nandini even more; she shouted, "Gayatri, enough, I am not a kid; look at me, I am already 25 and you are giving me a lecture on how to be careful about the traffic in Bangalore?"

Gayatri smiled and answered, "Dee, I am just trying to have a conversation with you; I know in what conditions you are travelling; I am just worried for you; that is it; I don't care if you cross the roads in Bangalore or choose to stay in a taxi." Both smiled over that.

Gayatri held Nandini's hand through the window and said, "Dear, remember when the devil keeps asking you to look at your past, there's something in your future he doesn't want you to see. Each morning, peace arrives at your door in the form of choices. Choose peace.".

Nandini gripped Gayatri's hand tighter, and a teardrop came rolling down Nandini's cheeks. This is what she was trying to avoid for so long; now nothing would stop Nandini from controlling her tears. She failed in concealing them, and all the flashbacks that she had suppressed came right in front of her. With a fake smile, she said bye to her best friend as the bus started writing new chapters in Nandini's life.

Nandini leaned over the window and heard the sound of rain. She had put on a jacket; the climate was cold, and due to the rain, the sky was not visible. Still, she was trying to search for something in that dark, empty, and thundering sky. Still, tears were flowing from the corner of her eyes; she did not want them to stop.

She had found comfort and warmth in those flowing tears. She always believed that rain was a sign of new beginnings, and as the bus moved forward, she felt a sense of hope and excitement for the future awaiting her. The sound of raindrops against the window became a soothing lullaby, calming her nerves and reassuring her that everything would be okay. She looked out of the window, and now she could see a hazy moon, not very clear, but she could make out that the moon was walking along with her. She said to herself, Thanks; at least you did not leave my side.

Nandini was a computer engineer, working for an IT MNC in Mumbai. Her dad was a businessman, and her mom was a loving and caring housewife. Dad loved her immensely, always supporting her decisions and encouraging her to excel in her career. Mom, on the other hand, was always there to provide emotional support and guidance whenever Nandini needed it. and she was her mom's best friend.

Nandini excelled in school and college; she always made her parents proud. There wasn't a single minute when Nandini didn't smile. She was the heart of the friends' group. Her jibber jabber never stopped; she gave life to all the non-living things around her. She was that adorable. In school, she excelled, then in engineering, she had a distinction, and finally, she got placed in an MNC in Mumbai through college placement.

Mumbai's vibes matched hers. Full of life, there is no difference between day and night; people are always energetic and on the move. Nandini loved Mumbai. She joined her new job, and she was happy doing whatever she was doing. In the meantime, she fell in love with Nirav.

Nirav was a colleague at her workplace, and they shared a strong connection from the beginning. Their love blossomed amidst the chaos of the city, making Nandini's life even more vibrant and fulfilling. Nirav was a very reserved kind of person; he hardly spoke to anyone. He was good at his work and kept to himself; he would go for coffee and smoke in breaks alone. First, Nandini felt how weird this guy was.

Nandini, being full of life and smiles, felt very annoyed by the behaviour of Nirav; she had hardly seen him smile or heard his voice; all the communication was through the system only, and that too was only work-related. Nandini took it upon herself as a challenge to change Nirav; she felt that fun was missing from his life. So, she set out on a mission to change Nirav.

Nandini started inviting Nirav to join her for lunch or after-work activities, hoping to bring him out of his shell. Despite his initial reluctance, Nirav eventually started opening up and showing a more playful side, much to Nandini's satisfaction. Nandini whispered in his ear, " Nirav, tum eise kyon ho, khadus jaise."?

That made Nirav smile broadly, and he answered back in her ear, "Eisa hi hu main." She said, "Paida hote hi"?

That made Nirav laugh out loud.

Both laughed loudly for the first time ever. Nirav said, Bye, Kaal milte hai. " And listening to this, all the other teammates shouted in unison, "Awwww..." Nirav and Nandini both blushed.

The next day, when Nandini came to the office, she went directly to Nirav's desk and said, "Khadus, Chal, let's have breakfast." Nirav declined. Then Nandini told him, "Dekh khadus, bhagwan ji ne mujhe mission pe bheja hai, unki galti sudharne ki " Nirav couldn't hide his smile. This is how slowly and gradually Nandini fell for Nirav.

Nirav finally agreed to have breakfast with Nandini, and as they sat together, he couldn't help but feel a warmth in his heart. The two of them shared a special bond that seemed to grow stronger with each passing day. It's a different case because Nirav never changed.

Despite Nirav's initial reluctance, Nandini's persistence and charm eventually won him over. Their unique dynamic continued to blossom, showcasing the power of their connection. This relationship was unlike any other for Nirav, as Nandini brought out a side of him that he never knew existed. Nandini, over the phone, had told Gayatri about Nirav. Gayatri advised her that, ok, Nandini, "it's always better to be in a relationship where you are loved. You are full of love and laughter; taking him as a lover shows that you love him, you light him up in this process but don't diminish your joyfulness." Nandini just dismissed the advice.

Nandini stayed in a flat; daily, she prepared breakfast for both and took it to the office, just to make Nirav happy. They roamed as a couple. Nandini seemed happy, so none of the friends went to tell her anything. To rethink: if he doesn't change?

One afternoon, while in the office, Nandini received a call from home saying her mom was not keeping well; it was her dad over the call. Nandini applied for leave and immediately went to her hometown. Her mom was very ill; her blood sugar had increased, and she had caught an infection. When she was shifted to the ICU later, her mom had pneumonia, and the chances of her mother's survival were very weak.

She would call Nirav from the hospital daily and give updates about her health. Nirav would only listen and say, "Don't worry, she will be fine." This was the first red flag in her relationship, which she ignored. She needed Nirav beside her, but she didn't dare to tell him so. Within the next two days, she lost her mom. The biggest shock Nandini and her dad had to face..

She expected Nirav to visit them, at least after hearing the news of the demise of her mom, but he didn't. She ignored that too, telling herself maybe he didn't get leave. She stayed with her father for a few days and then, after 15 days, joined work again.

When she met Nirav, she hugged him and started crying. Nirav got annoyed and said, Nandini, stop all this;

this is not the place to cry. People are staring. Nandini was shocked by this and stared at him with unbelievable anger. Then she asked him, "I needed you there, Nirav; why didn't you come?" Nirav said casually, What would I do if I came there? Nandini was taken aback by this answer.

She realised where she had landed with this wrong choice of hers. After this incident, a lot of arguments started taking place between Nirav and Nandini. She understood that Nirav was a self-centred person who hardly cared about anyone else's feelings. Whenever she confronted him, saying " Nirav, I love you so much, but can't you even lend your shoulders when I feel like crying? Am I asking too much?"

Nirav replied, " Nandini, I can't handle any of your drama; sometimes it becomes too much. I hate this crying and pacifying game. I can't do that; don't expect me to participate in any drama of yours. And excuse me; you were the one who came behind me asking for love. I am this way and will forever be this way only , stop trying to change me". This broke Nandini's heart.

First the loss of her mom, and now the heartbreak, she started slipping into depression. Looking at her condition, her boss asked her to take a break and go home for a few days. Here, Gayatri came to her rescue. Nandini cried her heart out in front of Gayatri.

She said I am done with life, Gayu; I see no hope in living a happy life hereafter. Dad is worried about my marriage, Nirav is distant from me, and I don't think there is any love or life left in my heart. Gayatri was listening carefully. She suggested to Nandini that if she wished, they could go to a past life regression therapist and see why certain things were happening in Nandini's life.

Nandini was sceptical about all this; she didn't believe in all this, but after Gayatri said, What's the harm in knowing? If you don't find it good, just think you heard a story and forget it. Nandini, after a lot of thought, said OK, but what do I need to do for that? I mean, what is the procedure? Any side effects or something I need to worry about?

Gayatri said, Let me book an appointment; you meet the regressionist and decide for yourself. If you don't feel good, let's abort the plan after listening to her. Nandini agreed. On the appointed date, Gayatri and Nandini went to meet the regressionist.

The lady, Mrs. Shah, was very warm and welcoming. Nandini was sceptical; sensing her discomfort, Mrs. Shah said, "I will tell you the procedure, and let me first assure you that there are no side effects of this modality. Mrs. Shah started by explaining how regression works and what to expect at the end of the session.

Mrs. Shah started explaining that: "First, tell us what issues you are facing so that we can focus on that issue only. Our soul carries all the information from all the lifetimes we have lived on earth. All the information is stored in the subconscious brain, which is difficult to access in a normal state.

When the client is sent into a trance by small hypnosis (without any drug or injection), the client can access the information from the storehouse of the subconscious. Instructions are given by the therapist, and the client can hear whatever is going on around them; they only need to focus on the instructions of the therapist and answer whatever questions the therapist is asking.

The client, according to their capacity, will be able to visualise or hear some information that is written down by the therapist, and when all the questions are answered, the therapist will safely bring the client out of a trance. Mrs. Shah also said that many times we get guidance from our spirit guides.".

Nandini and Gayatri nodded at each other, and Nandini said she was ready for the session. Nandini lay down comfortably, and Mrs. Shah asked her what issues she had and wanted to get the regression done for.

Nandini explained her relationship with Nirav; she told Mrs. Shah that I love him very much, but he never reciprocates in the same way; he doesn't even express what he feels; he always tells me, "Grow up, Nandini." I don't understand why he doesn't understand me and my love for him. So, I am eager to know what karmic connections we have with each other.

Mrs. Shah nodded and said, Let's start. Take a deep breath. Slowly and gradually, Nandini entered a semi-trance state, where she could hear questions asked by Mrs. Shah.

Mrs. Shah: Nandini Look down at your feet and feel the ground on which you are standing. What are you wearing on your feet? How is the ground beneath you?

Nandini has closed her eyes and made facial expressions as if she were trying to remember something. She said in a very low tone, "I can see a young girl standing on the banks of the Ganga; its pitch is dark."

Mrs. Shah: Do you recognise her?

Nandini: Yes, yes, it's me. It's me. I am standing on the bank of the Ganga.

Mrs. Shah: Pay attention; some will call out your name. Listen carefully.

Nandini went into deep silence; after a while, she said someone was calling my name; it's Dugga. Yes, Dugga, I am very scared tonight, Nandini said, as I am running away from my dad's house.

I am wearing a white sari with red borders, and my father is very powerful. Before he finds out, I have to reach the other side, rowing the boat.".

Mrs. Shah: Can you tell where you are going so hurriedly?

I am going to the other side of the river.

Nandini was again silent for a while, searching for the pictures to flash in front of her. Nandini narrated what she was seeing. Nandini said, "I have to reach the other side of the bank; I am in a hurry because I have run away from the house with the help of Mashi Maa (her caretaker).

Dugga is 16 years old, and tonight her love, Jagan, is waiting to get married to her on the other side of the banks.

I must reach there before my father's goons find me out. I am now rowing the boat. I am both scared and excited. As I reach the other side, I see Jagan waiting for me. I am smiling now. He is wearing a white kurta and a dhoti. I am so happy to see him. Baba has refused our marriage because he lives on the other side of the river. Baba said he is not a good match for you, so me and Jagan have decided to elope, taking advantage of the night.

Nandini kept silent for a long time. She was trying to identify something, which she was not able to do, so she said to Mrs. Shah, Ma'am Jagan is waiting for me; he has held my hand and said tonight we will marry and go away, leaving this village, so that your baba will never trace us. But Nandini kept quiet. Mrs. Shah asked: Do you recognise Jagan as anyone from this lifetime?

Nandini was puzzled; she nodded. No, I don't know him. I have never met him in this lifetime, but then why am I going with him and marrying him?

Mrs. Shah said, "Just go with the flow; see what your soul wants you to see at this very moment; don't judge; don't analyse; don't avoid getting the pictures; be calm; and feel what you have to feel. Later, we will analyse and discuss it. Now, continue telling me what happens next.

Nandini said I am very happy with Jagan; we both are getting married today, and his friends have arranged a small function. He is not wealthy like my dad, but I love Jagan very much. I feel he is my soulmate.

Mrs. Shah: "Let's move forward and come to the most important event of that lifetime.".

Nandini started crying loudly. No, please stop; don't hit him; it's not his mistake. Please listen to me. Nandini was sobbing, literally.

Mrs. Shah asked, "What is happening, Nandini?"?

Nandini started narrating: Baba sent the goons behind us when we were doing the marriage rituals. These goons came. We tried to run, but they held us. They are hitting Jagan very harshly. Jagan will die. Please leave him. These goons have held my hand tight. I am feeling helpless.

Jagan is beaten very badly. Ma'am, he is asking for water, but no one is giving him any. Jagan, through his pain, is trying to tell me, "Dugga, I will always come back for you; it's a promise."

The goons took me back to my house, where Baba slapped me and locked me in my room. I am sure Jagan must be dead by now. I am very depressed and angry.

Mrs. Shah instructed, " Nandini, go to the next most significant event of that lifetime.".

Nandini started narrating, "I am lying on the bed; I am very sick; I can't take the last picture of Jagan out of my head; from the day they locked me, I have given up food; I drink only water. I am vomiting blood; ma'am, I may die soon.".

Mrs. Shah exclaimed, Ah! What are your last thoughts while dying, Nandini?

Nandini said I was so unlucky in love; don't I deserve love?

Mrs. Shah allowed Nandini to close her eyes and lie down till all the memories sank back. Once she was okay, Mrs. Shah got Nandini out of her trance and asked her to drink water.

Mrs. Shah said, "I know you have too many questions to ask. But first, just relax. I will explain everything to you.

Mrs. Shah started explaining, "See Nandini, sometimes people come into our lives for a reason; they come to bring a storm into our lives or to just stir up emotions in our lives. In such a storm, we only get to know our strengths and weaknesses. So, Nirav has come into your life to stir the emotions inside you, to show you a mirror, to show where your weaknesses are, what you can handle, and what you can't.

They are like teachers to us; we should learn the lesson from the incident and not hold grudges against the person. Nirav definitely has some karmic connection with you, so he came into your life; also, he has come to teach you that you shouldn't be dependent on him for your happiness. You are complete with yourself. You are strong enough to hold your head high; why do you need any shoulders to lean on?

He taught you to be independent; silently thank him. And what we saw in the regression was about the lifetime where you didn't know who Jagan was. Your soul chose to show you this particular lifetime because it wants you to look forward and wait for Jagan to come into your life. Stop crying over the spilled milk. What had to happen? It happened . Remember Your soul mate must also be yearning for you somewhere because he has promised to come back to love you.

See, Nandini, we have two options: free will and destiny. Your free will can change your destiny. Don't feel helpless ever. God or higher energies never meddle with our free will.

The choice is yours.

SAYONEE: 2

The best day of your life is the one in which you decide that your life is your own.

No apologies or excuses. There is no one to lean on, rely on, or blame; the gift is yours; it is an amazing journey, and you alone are responsible for its quality.

This is the day your life really begins.

The bus reached Bangalore on time. Nandini got down, hired a taxi, and came to the apartment where she was allotted a flat by the company. She got out of the taxi and asked how much to pay; he replied in Kannada; she did not understand; she again asked him and told her in broken English; then she requested the driver to help her with the luggage, and he sounded rude.

That irritated Nandini, and both started arguing. Meanwhile, a young boy around twenty-nine came to Nandini's rescue. He asked, "hey snehetey, yen aaitu?"

(dear friend, what happened?) She said, Excuse me! He realised that Nandini had a problem with language, so he politely asked, "Ma'am, what happened?"?

She replied that the taxi driver was not helping with the luggage. The young boy, whose name is Neev, bent forward and whispered in her ear, "Never get into fights with ugly people; they have noticed,they have already lost in beauty . so they are always irritate" She just smiled. Now Neev went to the taxi driver and said the same sentence in Kannada; even he smiled. Sorry, madam. Neev called the security guard and asked him to help Nandini. Nandini said thanks and went away. Neev continued jogging.

Nandini joined her new office. She had changed; there was no smile on her face, and she looked lifeless. She spoke very little with everyone around her and stayed to herself. She had decided that she would only focus on her work and would not complicate her life by getting into any relationships. As of now, her mental state is not very good.

After the office, she used to come home by 5 p.m., have coffee, and after that Nandini had nothing much to do. Her cook suggested to Akka (sister in Kannada): Why do you not go down in the evening? There is a nice cool breeze; you will feel suffocated inside all day. Nandini said, Hmm, I will try that too.

That evening, she went down and sat on the bench in the park in her society. There was greenery everywhere, green and lush lawns, and Ashoka trees all around the building. She sat cross-legged on the bench, listening to old Hindi songs. In her mind, she thanked her cook for this suggestion. As soon as her thought was about to be over, a big plastic ball came and hit her head.

She looked here and there and found Neev and a little girl around 5 years old coming running towards her.

Neev and Pari stood in front of Nandini. Nandini was staring in anger at both. Neev said, "Shoot, I have taken my vitamins in the morning." "Pari, you didn't finish your milk, na. Now see, when this kuttima (name called out of love) scolds, it will hurt you the most. So, I drink milk and take vitamins. Nandini yelled, Stop your nonsense. "What if my head would have gotten injured?"?

Neev said, "Don't worry; from tomorrow, even if you start drinking milk, even if the ball hits, the pain will be less." Nandini asked Neev to shut up, threw the ball at Neev, and started walking back home. As Nandini turned, Pari went and held her hand and said, Sorry, we will be careful next time. Pari looked like an angel to Nandini. She bent down, kissed her, and said, It is ok, but tell your grown-up friend to look around while playing. Pari giggled and ran towards Neev.

Now it had become a daily routine that, after 30 minutes of Nandini's alone time, a ball came rushing towards her, and then she spoke to Pari for a while. Pari and Nandini started liking each other. Nandini would sit looking at the watch when 30 minutes would pass and Pari came to meet her.

One day, it was 45 minutes, and neither the ball nor Pari came to meet her. She felt worried and started walking towards the kid area, where she played daily with her older partner. Today, that older partner was also sitting on the bench silently. Nandini walked to him and asked, "Where is Pari? I am missing her." Neev said, "Me too ".

There was an awkward silence for a while, then Neev said, Sorry, we troubled you a lot. Nandini said it was ok; I like that trouble. This was the first time that Nandini had a direct conversation with Neev. She was a bold girl, but something was stopping her from investigating Neev's eyes. She avoided eye contact. She could not wait with Neev for long. She felt a magnetic pull towards him.

She hurriedly said bye and started walking towards her apartment. As she turned and started walking, she was trying to remember where she had seen those eyes, and why was she avoiding looking into them? As she walked further, she heard someone call her Durga from behind. There were chills running down her spine, and she had goosebumps. She felt as if Jagan had called her Dugga.

She turned back and saw Neev running towards her. Neev said, "You forgot your water bottle there'. Nandini asked," Why did he call her Durga?" He smiled sheepishly and said, "When the ball hit you on the first day and you were scolding me, I thought my god maa Durga ka avtar hai ye, so I and Pari called you Durga, ghussewali Durga." He said sorry and asked her not to tell Pari that he told Nandini about Durga.

Nandini's brain had almost stopped working now. She thought to herself, How is this possible? Is Neev, Jagan, which my soul has shown? How is that even possible? She tried brushing this thought away, but it kept coming back to her like a boomerang. She did not disclose it to anyone about Neev.

She could not wait or stop herself from meeting Neev daily; she took the opportunity to ask about Pari and strike up a conversation with Neev. One day she told Neev, "You know, I love to see you and Pari playing together. You become a kid with her. She is so comfortable around you. Nandini confessed that I feel jealous sometimes. I wish I could be small and with you people in a team.

Every time I see you, I just feel more alone." Ohhh, so "in isolationship," Neev laughed. Nandini just nodded. Nandini started liking Neev's company, and every evening they started meeting in the park. Nandini felt she had found someone just like herself. The light that was diminishing inside her started rekindling. She thought she found somebody just like herself, who was full of life and laughter.

Neev spoke so well, and Neev had so many things to say when Nandini listened attentively. They started loving each other's company. Once they were sitting on their regular bench, a ball came rushing towards them. Neev dogged the ball and said to Nandini, "Don't worry, I am here to take care of you "Nandini was not interested in what he was saying; she could only see his lips move.

Nandini thought to herself, "Neev, where were you for so many years? I got tired searching for you; if it were not for you, I would be so lost. I am so glad you came into my life. Can you picture it? Are you and I together? Never; we cannot be friends, anymore. I will always see you as something else. You changed me, Neev. I really didn't mean to love you so much."

Her chain of thoughts broke when Neev said, "Nandini, it stopped raining; let's go.".

Nandini refrained from expressing her feelings to Neev. She did not want to break her relationship with Neev, which was something precious to her.. She wanted to share the big news that she got the offer of pursuing higher education abroad from the company, which she was planning to decline. Also, today she firmly decided that she would share with him the past life regression visuals. And she wanted to tell Neev that Dugga had found her Jagan.

She came smiling, walking towards the bench. Her steps stopped, and her smile disappeared. She saw Neev sitting with Pari and a female. She tried to turn away, but Pari came running and hugged Nandini. Pari pulled Nandini and said, "Come, I will show you my mom." Nandini shrunk her eyebrows.

She felt a pang of jealousy . Despite her initial reluctance, Nandini followed Pari and the woman, curious to see who had taken her place in Neev's life. Nandini stood there like a statue when Pari introduced her to her parents, Mumma and Dadda. Nandini felt her heart breaking into pieces when Pari called Dadda to Neev. Nandini almost lost her understanding of what was going on. Two big teardrops were waiting to find their way out, from heart to eye.

She just said hi to Pari's mom, turned back, and started walking. Neev came running behind Nandini and said, Let me introduce you to my wife. As you are on an isolation ship, I am on a separation ship. He tried to cover the pain on his face. Pari stays with me for a few days when her mom travels out of the station.

Nandini smiled deceitfully and said, "If I had known things would end up this way, I'd have never..." That is okay. I just came to tell you that I have been selected to study abroad, and I will be leaving in a few days. I wanted to share this happiness with you.

Congratulations on being selected to study abroad! I'm sure you will have an amazing experience. Just remember, distance doesn't change the bond we share. (Neev couldn't even manage to say this much.) He just said congratulations and all the best. They would both try to be happy without each other. At least, that is what they were trying to tell themselves.

FREEWILL OR DESTINY, WHAT SHOULD THEY CHOOSE? ON THE CROSSROADS. They just had to believe in their decisions.

IRSHA

The law of karma states unequivocally that though we cannot see the connections, we can be sure that everything that happens to us, good and bad, originated once in something we did or thought. We are responsible for what happens to us, whether or not we can understand how. It follows that we can change what happens to us by changing ourselves; we can take our destiny into our own hands.

This is a story about how we judge a book by its cover. What we see with our two eyes may not be the true story of what is actually behind it all. We humans are too quick to judge, and jump to conclusions. To explain what my point is, here goes a story.

There was a dense forest in central India. Many of the monks had given up their materialistic lives and dedicated their lives to devotion to Lord Vishnu. They stayed in the forest, ate fruits, and slept in the jungle, among the mosquitoes and fear of wild animals. One night after their meditation, they sat alongside the campfire and started discussing how their beloved Lord Vishnu gave darshan to a 5-year-old Druva. (Druva was also a devotee of Lord Vishnu.). These monks were so jealous that they started saying Lord Vishnu was biased and was neglecting all of these monks. They were going through so much pain and suffering, sleeping in the jungle, among the animals, and God was being partial towards that 5-year-old kid. Narada, the 'celestial being' overheard what was being said about his master. He could not hold it in his stomach for long and immediately went to Vaikuntha loka and confronted Lord Vishnu.

Narada muni said to Lord Vishnu, "Bhagwan, I cannot believe what your devotees are saying about you."

The LORD said, "Tell me; I will answer.

Narada said," Bhagwan, even I felt that, so I will complain too, How can you give sakshyat darshan to little devotee Druva and not to these monks who have been in this forest for so many years?"

The LORD just smiled and said, OK, do one thing, tell all my devotees to meet at one place and go towards the river; there will be a boat waiting for them with a boatsman. Narada said, Shall I accompany them? The LORD said, Sure, don't forget to absorb the beauty of nature. Listening to his master, Narada went excitedly to the forest to share the news. He told the monks that he conveyed their plea to the Lord and came back with a solution. They will have to walk a certain distance and then get into a boat. The Lord had arranged a surprise for them.

All of them got into the boat. The sailor did not say a word. He was rowing northward as if he knew where he had to take them all. As the sun kissed the mountains, it felt as if his breath was blown into the earth. The mountains were green, the water was clear, and the stones were heavy and grey. Everything looked beautiful. As they moved further, they saw a white mountain. It sometimes looked white, grey, and sometimes orange, depending on the placement of the sun. Suddenly, Narada remembered what the LORD had said about absorbing nature. Narada could not resist but asked the sailor What's that huge mountain? And how come it is changing colors? Is it cladded with snow, but it doesn't look like one.

Sailor said, Don't you know about this mountain? " All said, in union, "no.". This is the famous mountain called "DRUV MOUNTAIN ". This mountain is made up of all the bones of the devotee of Lord Vishnu named Dhruv, not from one life but from thousands of lives till he got the sakshyat darshan of LORD VISHNU. All the devotees were awe-struck. Narada too.

When others succeed, you should be happy. If they can do it, so can you. The success of others does not, in any way, lessen your chances of succeeding. If anything, it should motivate you to keep pushing forward. Jealousy only eats up your beauty. Have more faith in yourself; you have something that other people don't. Jealousy actually pulls us down spiritually. All the practices and sadhana that we do and still have seeds of jealousy inside us are like weeds in the garden of flowers, taking nutrition from healthy sadhana.

The meaning of karma is in the intention. The intention behind the action is what matters. Those who are motivated only by the desire for the fruits of action are miserable, for they are constantly anxious about the results of what they do.

Lastly, let us understand what the difference is between karma and bhakti (devotion)

Karma: sitting, standing, walking, singing, dancing, talking, cooking, studying, working, giving, taking, eating, sleeping, etc

Bhakti: sitting, standing, walking, singing, dancing, talking, cooking, studying, working, giving, taking, eating, sleeping, etc. for the beloved LORD with SAMARPAN.

For God, all his devotees are equal. He is not interested in taking any test of yours to see whether you love him or not. He is self-sufficient in himself. We do tapasya, we do japa, we do vrat, and we do puja. We want to purify ourselves and make ourselves capable of standing in front of him. We say don't eat nonveg and go to the temple. We consider ourselves impure to stand in front of that maha Shakti. But does God really peep into your belly to check what you had before you came to the temple, or does he peep into your heart, which is full of devotion or not?

I am not encouraging anyone to eat nonveg and visit temples, because I know and have been to some of the temples where, even if you are wearing a dress or carrying a handbag in which you ever carried or consumed nonveg and you are wearing it without washing it, you are sure to get into some big trouble. Those temples belong to the Nath Panthis. I had the grace to visit Revansidh Mandir in Satara district, Maharashtra. I have heard so many stories about this mandir that those who eat non- veg or drink alcohol and take darshan, usually meet with an accident. Now, this is not because God doesn't like it. Let us understand some rishis like discipline, that are to be followed in school. No exemption for any student. So some temples have some rules to maintain, keep the purity and satvikta of the surroundings, no compromise can be accepted. And as educated citizens, instead of arguing, we must support the management. Respect the rules of each tradition. Don't play with the traditions, because many times we don't know what energies we are dealing with.

All I mean is to have a heart full of love and compassion for others.

ELIXIR OF LIFE: (AMRIT)

From time immemorial, Gods as well as demons have been crazy to find the amrit and be immortal. As mentioned in the Vishnu Puran itself, the churning of the ocean was to bring the Amrit out of the ocean so that Gods could consume it and become immortal. We know that with birth, only we carry the seed of death inside us. Each day that seed is growing, we are nearing death. Even the Gods who walked this earth plane could not escape their deaths. Ravana, a well-read Brahmin king (not by his caste, I am mentioning, I am appreciating his wisdom), too dreamt to be immortal, so he tied up all the 9 planets in the lock-up so his astrological chart should not be disturbed.

I want to ask a simple question: If given a choice, would you like to be immortal? Ok, I'll give you the choice too. You will never have a shortage of money; in short, you will live like a king. Will you take the offer? Ya, ya, you will be young too. (Who would like to be an old king?)

Now I will tell you a story that I heard from my neighbour in Daman. This family originally belonged to Gorakhpur, Uttar Pradesh. We moved into that apartment around the same time as this Gorakhpur family moved in. Let us call them Sharma. They stayed on different floors, and we were different. We frequently met at functions. But at every function, I noticed that other ladies were gossiping about Sharma's. Still, I hadn't made any new friends, so I did not get to know what they were all gossiping so much about. In the meantime, the only odd thing that I noticed was that their family members' ages ranged from max 100 to min 12, which was something I could not understand. Many times, I thought maybe guests stayed with them. They were quite a family.

One fine evening, one of their sons, Sachin, who was around 30 years old, came to my house with a 12-year-old boy and said, Madam?

I said, Come in, what can I do for you?

Sachin said, This is Prince, my little brother; he scored low marks last semester; please, can you take his tuition?

It was very awkward for me to say no; I had just left the lectureship, and since teaching was my passion, I said yes.

From the next day on, tuition classes started regularly. He was doing well. He hardly spoke; he was an introvert, and I did not know whom to talk to about his matters in his house; his dad was never available; his mom did not know anything other than Bhojpuri; his elder brother was much more introverted and shy than him; his Bhabhi was in ghunghat all the time; and I was new to all the family members. I decided I would only handle him, and his no complaints would go home.

After Diwali, one evening Prince's mom came home and started saying something in Bhojpuri. She seemed excited. It took me a while to understand what she was saying. I said, Amma, come and sit inside. She sat down, and I listened to her carefully. She was saying today we have our biggest festival, "CHATT." I want you to come with us; go get ready. I managed to only understand this much. I went inside and got ready with a blank mind. I had never heard anything about Chatt's going with my students' families to experience a beautiful lesson.

That evening, we females were dumped into a car and droven towards the beach. For the first time, I saw so many fruits, sugar cane, and sweets. Moreover, beautiful women in sindoor and bangles are singing folk songs, carrying puja stuff over their heads, and standing in water, facing the sun. Marvelous. Just Marvellous. “Jai chatti maiyaa " While I was sitting on the shore, some of the prince's relatives pointed out that I was not one of them. one asked me, “ Aap prince ki teachrwa" (are you, prince teacher?)

I said yes.

She further asked, " aapka babuwa nahi huwa abhi? Biha hoke kitna saal hua? (don't you have children yet? How many years have you been married?

I said no, I don't have children yet. It's been 8 years since our marriage.

Listening to this, she came close to me. Held my hand and said, Listen,SO only I think Amma bought you here. I will tell you something, ok, but don't tell Amma that I told you this. First, promise me that you will not be sad. See this CHATTI MAIYYA is very merciful. Mark my words, by next year you will come here with your babu. And about the secret come close I will tell you, She pulled me close and stared: "You know that Bhudhiya in Amma's house? I said yes, Prince Dadi. She said yes. You know what happened to her? I nodded my head left to right. She whispered in my ears. " she had died when she was young, around 40, she had no children also. All the relatives had gathered. She had 5 sisters, all of whom had come rushing to see her for the final time. Her Nadi was checked. Pyre was prepared, she was taken till there in procession and when she was kept on pyre she suddenly woke up screaming Where is my tobacco? Give my tobacco? All were scared like hell. She was brought home and given water.

She later told everybody that she had died and felt like she was moving through some tunnel towards some light. At the end of the tunnel, she found her clan God waiting for her and saying that her time was not up yet. He said, "You have to raise the kids and grandkids. You have a very, very long and healthy life. Go and enjoy. Don't Worry, you will never be sick.". She kept saying to her husband, I am over 40. How will we have a baby now?, But nature always thinks ahead of us. She had a healthy male child at the age of 55, and after a few years, 5 grandchildren and 4 great-grandchildren. Price's dadi was more than 100 years old.

The lady was still telling me that Amma loves her mother-in-law a lot. She does her sewa with her whole heart, Lucky is that old day to have a daughter-in-law like Amma. But you know that these days she is troubling Amma a lot? I said, but she is blessed that she will never fall ill, na? then what trouble? That lady said: "That Granny sits cursing God, şaying why the hell did you give me such a long life", Please take me away.

I asked, "Why?"

She said, "Areeeee. DIDI, you only think na, the people who were born during her time are all gone now; forget that even the immediate next generation to her , half are dead, half are sick, and all her younger siblings are dead. Her husband is dead. Her son has grown old. The house is full of children, noise, TV, and mobile devices. Conversation and language are such that she is not able to understand. She is not able to go up and down the lift. She wants to go back to the village, but they cannot take her there as she can't board the flight and there are no relatives of her age in the village. That is making her angrier and, in return, cursing God for giving her a long life."

That evening, looking at the setting sun, looking at all the women carrying the sieve on their heads submerged in water and praying to the setting sun, I was thinking to myself, maybe they are all praying and saying in union " THANK YOU GOD FOR A LIFE LIKE SUNRISE AND SUNSET. NOT TOO LONG NOT TOO SHORT. PERFECT JUST AS TO EXPERIENCE ALL THE RIGHT TASTE OF EMOTIONS FROM SWEET TO SOUR TO SPICY."

And yes, chatti maiyya did call me next year again with my babuwa.

KARMA VERSUS DHARMA

Do you think that human ethics are learned or natural? My actions are my only true belongings. I cannot escape the consequences of my actions. My actions are the ground on which I stand. - Thich Nhat Hanh

Looking at the above wise words again, the word "karma" comes to mind.

Basically, there are three types of karma

Kriyaman (present action or karma yet.to be created). A simple example is that you are feeling thirsty and are about to get up and drink water.

The second type of karma is **sanchita** karma (accumulated or dormant) . An example of this would be Gandhari's 100 sons dying in the Kurukshetra War.

[The story goes like this, after the war in Kurukshetra was over, Krishna went to meet Gandhari and Dhritarashtra.

Gandhari came running to Krishna and started crying loudly, asking, What did you get from this war? Can't you see the blood everywhere? Tell me, who is happy now? Drishrastratra came and joined hands in front of Krishna and asked Krishna, Gopala, why are all 100 of my sons dead and all of Kunti's five Pandavas alive? Why isn't even my one Kaurava alive? Krishna made the king sit down and told him that this is his sanchita karma, which he has been carrying for uncountable lifetimes. King asks how and why. Krishna tells him that many lifetimes before Dhritarashtra was a hunter, he was just roaming in the jungle, Then he got tired, and while he was taking rest under a tree, he heard the noise of birds chirping but was unable to bear that because of the chirping sound coming from the neighbouring tree. As a result, he got angry and burned the entire tree.

There were 100 little eggs of the bird, and the bird cursed, saying that you will also lose all your kids and will cry helplessly like me. After that, you took many births but in none of the lifetimes you had the luck of having 100 children together, so your Sanchit Karma had to patiently wait for so many lifetimes to give you this ripened fruit.]

The third type of karma is the **prarabdha** (already on the way to deliver the ripe fruits of our karma depending on whether they are good or bad.

Have you wondered who keeps track of all this karma?

The nine planets keep the accounts of our karmas and on the day the baby is born the screenshot is taken of the positions of all the planets, and the information is downloaded and made into a janam kundali. what we call modern-day astrology. But if destiny is already decided, then where does our free will come into play?

This story will surely make us think deeply about destiny and free will. Through this story, let's try to learn who wins free will or destiny. It's an open-ended question; don't jump to conclusions so easily.

Ram Ram! I am Madhav Rao Deshmukh. Today I turned 80 years old, and here I want to tell you all the secrets that I had thought I would take to the grave. But what the ancestors said is very true. You can't take anything into the grave, not even guilt or love, whatever you have spent it all here and gone totally empty hearted then only you will have a grand welcome in the heavens.

So, what do you think I am carrying in my heart? Ok, you will guess at the end of the story. This story belongs to the pre-independence era.

We Deshmukhs are the landlords from the Satara district. Our lands are far stretched, and wherever your eyes go, we are the landlords. But you know what happens in the landlord's house? The landlord rules the house too, and others are just like his servants. My dad had three brothers, the elder was the boss of the house, the middle brother helped the elder brother with his petty work; and my father was a devotee of Lord Vithala. He would only sing bhajans and would walk to Pandharpur Wari on foot twice a year to meet his beloved god. My father was a simple man, and my mother was too; they had no say in any decisions of the family matters, and they hardly looked after me and my elder brother.

My brother knew at a very young age that we had to do something on our own to be successful in life because if we stayed here for long, we would be serving the elder uncle only, and we would also have no penny in hand.

For us, going to secondary school was also a challenge, we had to walk 3 km up and down, had no proper food, torn uniforms, which mom used to patch wherever they tore, and rubber slippers. But my other cousins were far better, we understood this partiality but there was none to raise the voice for us. After my brother finished his matriculation, he searched for a job in Pune, left the village for the job and promised me that he would also pull me out as soon as I finished my matriculation. He kept his promise, called me Pune, and admitted me to Diploma College. We both did not have money as we both had to work daytime and attend night classes. Many times, we had to sleep only on tea and buns from an Iranian café. But we were both determined to study well and settle down well. There were not many hopes to get our parents to bring us to stay with us; they were very content staying there. They had very little need, they were not exposed to comfort, and above all, they wanted to live among their own people.

My parents had a very pure heart, they never judged, they did not find any partiality; and they did not see the treatment as unfair in the house. They were as innocent as the newly born child. But we were not, we could see the difference; we had ambitions, and we also wanted to grow, just did not want to remain as slaves under the name of Deshmukh. We had to create our own identity. And we were walking that path now. Gopal Rao Deshmukh had finished his bachelor's degree and moved to Bombay for further education. Every month, he used to send me some money orders and some to our baba also back home. My uncles were happy with what we were doing but not very proud because they had lost four hands that would work like labourers in the field.

And finally, the money we are earning will be our money, nothing will go to them, so they showed total disinterest in us. There were three other cousins who were growing up with us. Only Gopal Rao was a bit older, and we were all of the same age. Gopal Rao, during his studies at Bombay College, found a soul mate and decided to marry her and settle down in Bombay. He sent a letter by post informing them of the same. Nobody was happy about this decision, but nobody could do anything either. Because of this one move, Gopal Rao and the other three, Bhagwant Rao, Manohar Rao, and I were in trouble.

Since the elders of the family had started looking for the brides for all three of us without our knowledge,. I was in Pune working as a civil engineer after my diploma. Bhagwant was in Nashik, and Manohar was in the village, looking after the fields.

In the olden days, much importance was given to the family's reputation. Once they gave the surname, the next question was which place? Once the place name is known, surely some or another relative is present in that family, and then it is considered a reputed "khandani" (clan) family. So, in those days, keeping the reputation of the family was very important. It is not limited to how the young girls behave or whether the women take veils on their heads or not, but also whether men keep their word or not. If you have promised something, it must be done if you are a real khandani. "Pran jaye par vachan na jae". (Life goes, but promises do not.).

So, one such Sunday, a few wiser men were gathered in the footsteps of a temple and chewing tobacco, when one old man said, Deshmukh Savkar, Gopala got married in the city, but we missed out on the big function over here, But don't worry, the other old man interrupted; three more parties are still pending.

The best thing about Deshmukh's party is the band and the horse dance. My eyes never get tired of seeing that. The third fellow dived in, saying, You know how much it costs for a horse to dance all night? That only Deshmukh can do, and the bride we must choose for them must have their equality, not anyone can be Deshmukh's daughter-in-law. Softly, one wiser old man said mothe (big) Savkar. I know of landlords just like yours; they are Gaekwad from Sangli, a big joint family, but they are very humble people. I heard they even have many young boys and girls of marriageable age. I suggest just casually visiting and coming if you can. Deshmukh Savkar said thank you, baba and left for home.

He thought about this for two days, then he took his middle brother and said, Let us go and visit the Gaekwads. His brother asked what we would say if they asked why we were there? We will tell them honestly, and then we will fix the date and get the function done. The younger brother was reluctant, but they came to the Gaekwad's haveli (residency). It was a huge one. They had come in a bullock cart; they were welcomed with jaggery and water. Women were not allowed out. Then the head of Gaekwads, Tatyasaheb, came out and asked the reason for the sudden visit, Deshmukh explained everything in detail, and the conversation went on for quite a long time. It went so deep that they found that knots had been tied between their ancestors as well.

All in all, it was a successful meeting. It was then decided that Sunday was an auspicious day and Bhagwant Rao would be having a holiday,so he could come and they could all o see the bride.

Sunday had arrived; there was a festive-like atmosphere in Gaekwad's haveli, as Deshmukh was coming to see their beloved "Vaijanta.". Well, there were three more cousins of Vaijanta of the same age, which means marriageable age, but Tatyasaheb, after meeting Deshmukh Savkar, said only our Vaijanta can survive in that big house, so let them see Vaijanta. God knows if that prophecy of Tatyasaheb was true or if he was really that wise to understand the strictness and shrewdness of Deshmukh Savkar.

Vaijanta was a 15-year-old girl and very intelligent compared to her other cousins. She did well in school, too. She was not a shy girl at all; she would listen to two and give back four in return. She was a very straightforward girl, a straight thinker. She was of average height and an average-looking girl from a village who was not very fancy. However, she knew all the household chores, such as cooking and cleaning.

The respected Deshmukhs arrived in the haveli. Males were made to sit in the open space where the tent was put up for shade, while Gaekwad did not want to show they were any less in terms of royalty. Females were taken inside the house. All were served tea and poha (flattened rice made with chilli). As soon as the refreshment was over, the older men in the Deshmukh family started hurrying and started saying that the muhurta (auspicious time) was nearing, Get the girl ready and bring her out. Let us not miss the muhurta; it will be inauspicious to miss it. All the women inside were whispering something into each other's ears, nothing was audible to anyone.

There were nearly 30 Deshmukh men and 15 Gaekwad men standing and staring at that little 15-year-old girl. As I said, she was not very tall; she was wearing her grandmother's nine-yard silk green sari that made her look like a doll rolled in a cloth and brought out. Her little hands were managing to keep the veil on the head properly so that it did not fall 100 times in front of all.

Taking baby steps as it was highly difficult to walk with a nine-yard sari. Somehow, she reached the spot. She was not allowed to look up at all. She was also not allowed to sit on a chaupat (baithak) , a low-level stool, until told by some elders. Her tests would be starting soon. She was standing so nervous that, with her toenail, she was trying to dig the earth and try to escape from there if possible. She was just hearing the random voices saying, You ask, no-no you ask first, is it your honour, you ask, and so on, but no one was asking. She was about to say, Shall I leave? when she heard a very stern voice asking her questions. Little one, what is your full name?

Vaijanta: "Vaijanta Bhausaheb Gaekwad"

Till then, someone else started asking, "Can you cook?"

Vaijanta: "Yes"

Can you stitch?

Vaijanta: "Yes" was her answer.

Then someone in the crowd said, if we ask everything, what will the women ask?

They said okay.

Vaijanta, you can go inside. She got up from the seat, bowed down three times to the entire guest to ask for their blessings, and went inside. Meanwhile, Bhagwant

Rao's friend asked, How did you find her? Bhagwant Rao said annoyingly, You can marry if you want.

Vaijanta was taken to the room where all the Deshmukh ladies were sitting. There, she was made to sit between all the females, and she was asked all types of questions. Like, can you cook bhakri? Can you cook puranpoli? Will you stop eating non-vegetarian food if tomorrow your husband decides to leave it? Show the shape of your feet [because it is a superstition that flat legs are not good for the bride] Walk and show, so that we know you have no disability, sing and show, so that we know your pronunciations are not flawed. That poor soul Vaijanta was almost in tears, but she was rescued by her grandmother, who said that meals were ready; please have the meals first.

After the heavy meals, both male family members sat down for discussion, having the paan (betel leaf). Gaekwads were very anxious as to what would be the outcome, it was not about status or anything as both were equally rich, but Deshmukhs were a bit far away and their cultures were also different. They seemed to be an educated family.

Deshmukh said to Tatyasaheb, We like everything about your family—the simplicity, honesty, and hospitality. You have given us no reason to say no. We can go ahead with the alliance. Tatyasaheb said, At least take the opinion of the son-in-law. Deshmukh Savkar laughed and said we do not have such weak sanskaras, unlike others. Yeah, and another thing, about the dowry

Tatyasaheb, Deshmukhs have never held their hand in front of anyone; please let it be such that it suits the status. The last line somewhere pricked in the heart of Tatyasaheb, but he did not speak to anyone.

After reaching home, Bhagwant Rao threw a big tantrum. By then, he was working in the Nashik Municipal Market and thought himself a big shot because of his father, Deshmukh Savkar. Bhagwant told his dad that he disliked the girl, and he utterly refused to marry her at any cost. His father was upset with this. He said that he couldn't go back on his words. Do whatever, but you have to get married to her. Maybe I will get you married to another girl of your choice after a year or two. [In those days, two marriages were allowed among Hindus]. Bhagwant Rao refused this offer too, packed his bag, and left for Nashik. He said, Do whatever you want, and don't force me to marry that girl.

Now, Deshmukh Savkar was in a big fix, with what face was he going to face and say no to the Gaekwads. This act would ruin the reputation of their watandari and their status in society. He had lost his sleep over this matter as the marriage date was coming near. In the house, nobody had the guts to say anything in front of Savkar other than his youngest brother, because he had already surrendered himself to God, so he had no fear or expectations from anyone. He went to his elder brother and said, Dada why are you suffering so much in vain? This world is just an illusion; If Vithala closes one door for us, he will surely open another one for us. You need not be disappointed at all. Savkar got furious and asked if his Vithala could solve this marriage jumble? The youngest said yes, Vitthala will solve it. What if Bhagwant Rao said no? My son, Madhav Rao will be ready for this marriage, this is my word to you.

You don't have to stop any of the marriage preparations. Both the brothers hugged each other tightly, whereas Madhav Rao in Pune had no slightest idea that his marriage was arranged and preparations were going on. Nobody bothered even to inform him. Marriage preparations were going on at very high speed on both sides. Gaekwads had been to Belgaum to buy gold ornaments for the bride and also silk saris. The women of the house were busy making sweets. Back in those days, brides had to give so many sweets that the sweets should be distributed in an entire village in each house and also to the guests who had attended the wedding.

There were no catering services. Weddings were usually held in small temples in the evening. Everything was running smoothly in Gaekwad's house; everything was in place and timely. There was only one week remaining, and now real confusion had started in Deshmukh's house. Madhav Rao's father sent a telegram to Pune saying that some emergency had come and he needed to come to Satara immediately. Madhav Rao, after receiving the telegram, thought about all the worst things that could possibly happen to make him panic about the situation, so he prepared himself for all the worst scenarios possible. As he was approaching his house wearing bell bottoms, thinking the worst thoughts in his mind, he found nothing suspicious or unusual; rather, he saw some festive celebrations going on.

Women are singing loudly, making edibles, and whatnot. He directly went to his elder uncle, bowed down, touched his feet, and said, What is going on? What is a happy occasion in this house? Is that why Baba sent me the telegram to come quickly? His elder uncle was silent; he was not in a position to answer, Then his baba came and said congratulations Madhava we have seen you a bride and your marriage is next week.

Madhav Rao stood up shockingly and said, baba, how could you do this? I haven't seen her. I am an engineer; will I be able to adjust to her? Will she adjust to me? Baba, at least allow me to see if I like her or not. Madhav's baba said, "This all is in vain, dear; your mother's and my marriage were fixed even before we were born, and word is a word. What if you were blind, ugly, or limping? Do you think I would not marry her? I would surely marry her because, for me, my father's word is a command, and I wouldn't dare to argue. Now you decide: my sanskaras win or your arrogance?

Madhav Rao gave in and got ready for the marriage. He was not happy at all, but with a grumpy face, he arrived for the marriage. The news of the groom's exchange was told to the Gaekwad a few days ago only because they should not feel cheated and, if they want, they can break the alliance.

Both, being reputed and respected families, did not opt to take such a drastic step. In those days, marriages were done between families; the reputation of the family was of utmost importance. Even Vaijanta was ok with the changed groom, as she had not seen the first one either, so what difference would that make anyway? She laughed to herself.

The marriage took place in the evening. Madhav Rao didn't smile that entire day. Vaijanta was in her new navvari saree, full of gold jewellery, looking like a gold doll, cute and beautiful. A bride, who was going to her house bag full of dreams, eyes full of imagination, and all mixed emotions.

How will the members of the family treat me? What should I call each family member? Will they love whatever I cook? Will I become homesick? What if I feel sick, whom should I tell all this? Damn, so many questions in this little brain while traveling in the bullock cart.

Finally, they reached their haveli, and the women of the house who had reached early came with the Aarti-thali and started rotating Aarti around the faces of bride and groom, it's for the reason that no evil forces should stay with them, and seeing this light, they will run away. Later, they had dinner and both slept in different rooms. Newlyweds are not allowed to sleep together until Satya Narayan puja is conducted at home.

After two days, pujas were going to be conducted. Till then, Vaijanta had won the hearts of many of them in the house. Two times she even went to Madhav Rao to ask for tea, but he just walked off. Then she commented, Next time, make your own tea if you want.

On the morning of Satya Narayan puja, they play a game called "rang pani." The big bowl is taken, milk is poured, some rose petals are thrown, and a ring is thrown in that bowl. The bride and groom, who are sitting across from each other, have to put their right hand inside and find the ring. One who finds the ring is the winner and is considered dominant over the other.

In this game, Vaijanta won... She won. She was so happy. In the afternoon, the Satya Narayan puja was over, lunch was served, and after lunch, Madhav Rao went to his room, packed his bags, and said, I am leaving for Pune. All were shocked. His aunt came running and started asking, Are you on your senses? What are you talking about? The urguncy means I am leaving alone; you know right, you were married three days ago. She is your wife now. You can't leave her this way.

Madhav Rao said: "You all married her to me for your convenience and for your reputation, so she becomes your responsibility, not mine. " He said this and just walked away."

Vaijanta heard the conversation; she felt heartbroken, and she cried near her mother-in-law. She continued crying for days. She was her father-in-law's favourite; she cried even in front of him, saying, Why is my fate so bad? Has no happiness ever been written in my life? Father-in-law would always say, girl:God can't be so ruthless; this is your testing time; have patience; see good days will surely come.

Whenever she cried in front of Deshmukh Savkar, he would say, Bala (baby) if you don't like it here, please go back to your place. We will come back when Madhav Rao is ready. She used to get annoyed and say, baba I am the daughter-in-law of this house, and only my dead body will leave from here. My husband's absence is not my choice. I will think he is a Sainik (army) working for the borders of India, but I will not leave this house at any cost. You all have given me love and care as much as they do in my own house, so why should I stay there like a refugee leaving my own house. Yes, my husband is out of his senses, but surely someday he will understand that life can't be spent alone.

One year went by; Madhav Rao had come for Diwali. He had bought a sari for his aunts and one for Vaijanta. That was enough to make her happy. There was no spoken conversation between them. Vaijanta only used to write inland letters to him, telling him about what she did on the farms, how many cows were there, how many liters of milk they gave, and so on. She hardly got any reply.

But that was also enough to keep the fire kindling. There in Pune, Madhav Rao was doing very well as a civil engineer. Soon he got a government post in Goa, and he was transferred to Goa. Madhav Rao was a workaholic. Vaijanta had accepted her fate and was busy looking after the house, after Deshmukh Savkar, if anyone was powerful, it was Vaijanta.

Savkar was very soft with her. She was like her daughter to him. She used to take care of all his medical needs. He has started being sick most of the time now. It has been almost 10 years now since Madhav Rao and Vaijanta stayed separate.

He visited the village to meet the other members of the family but hardly spoke to her. It has become a habit for her now. She didn't even care much.

One summer afternoon, Deshmukh Savkar was almost breathing his last breath. Everyone knew that. He had sent a telegram to Mumbai and Goa to call both brothers. He was holding Vaijantas's hand and crying as if saying, Please forgive me if you can. The words were not clear, nor could anyone hear them, as everyone was thinking that he was crying in pain.

But actually, what happens is that during the time of death, our entire life flashes in front of our eyes like a movie. We get to review what good and bad we have done all throughout our lives, but now what is the use? As we can't rectify anything, all we have to do is repentance and guilt, and that brings us to tears, not physical pain.

Till Madhav Rao and Gopal Rao reached Satara, Deshmukh Savkar had already left the world. The body was taken to the cremation ground, and the Agni (fire) was given, but the next big ritual was left, called the pinda-daan (a post-death ritual in Hinduism). In this, food is offered to the dead. And the food has to be accepted by the crow; if the crow accepts it immediately, it means the soul has no remaining wishes. It was a contented soul. This ritual is taken very seriously because there can't be any foul play in it.

Many times, there are plenty of crows hovering over the cemetery, but even after the food is kept by their names, the crows refuse to eat it. They keep hovering over it but don't touch it. This means the soul surely has some wishes remaining. If the crow doesn't touch then, the same prasad is given to the dog; sometimes even a dog sniffs and goes away without eating,. the same prasad is given to a cow if the cow doesn't eat then sure it is a bad omen, and some other rituals need to be performed to bring peace to the soul.

But the case of Deshmukh Savkar was not that bad. When the Prasad was offered to the crow, no crow came to touch it. Then the priest suggested that if anyone has hurt the dead soul, knowingly or unknowingly, please ask for forgiveness. A few of them came forward, including his brother Manohar, his son Bhagwant Rao, and a few people from business. Still, the crows didn't move an inch.

Then suddenly Deshmukh Savkar, the youngest brother, came to Madhav Rao and said, see, Madhava your uncle loved Vaijanta like his daughter, I know surely his life is staying back in her, worrying what will happen to her, till he was alive she was protected after him. Who will look after her? I am also aging now, and I can't promise to take care of her. You had your own way for 12 years now, at least for your uncle's soul peace, go and promise your uncle that you will look after her. She is a good girl Madhav, otherwise, who would live in this house without a husband for 12 years?

Madhav Rao did not speak a word, went near the ashes, took water and basil leaves in his hands, and said lost kaka. I lost, sansakars won. I am sorry for my behaviour. I promise to take Vaijanta as my wedded wife and will take her with me wherever I go on duty.

The moment he finished saying this, the crow, the dog, and the cow were fighting over Prasad. That indicated how happy the soul was after listening to the promise, and he knew Madhav Rao would never break it.

After this incident, I had a very beautiful and fulfilling life. I am blessed with.....three children and all are doing exceptionally well. Now I am free of guilt and by sharing this story I am sharing the formula that I wasted 12 years without love, you don't commit the same mistake. Show your love, express it before it's too late.

KARMA VS. DHARMA EXTENSION

Do you know when a man feels totally helpless? Not when he goes through a financial crunch or loses a loved one, but when he himself is on the death bed. It is not only his physical condition that is bothering him, but more than that, when he is lying on the bed, he finds plenty of time to reflect on what he has and what he has not done in his life. In those moments when the person recalls, reflects, and introspects, he understands how helpless he is now that he can't undo the wrong things he has done in his life. So it becomes very necessary to live with awareness. Pause and reflect before we react; pause before we speak ill; pause before we talk bad about others. Remember, one day we are all going to be breathing our last. That is inevitable. And the guilt of loving less while alive is unbearable. And we think that after death, everything is over, but we are wrong. As family members, we should and must help them to reduce these negative feelings even after death. They communicate with us even after they die; they try to express how they are feeling. It's said their soul has been around us for 13 days. It's during this time that we can still pray for a peaceful journey forward.

I would like to narrate an incident about my mother. My mother died at the age of 55. It was a very big loss for us siblings as well as my father. We had two sisters who were married, and one sister and one brother were yet to be married. We, two sisters, are blessed with one child each. It was the month of April, and we had a call from the father's dad saying mom was critical and admitted. So all four siblings gathered in my hometown; she was in the ICU. All were not allowed to meet her at the same time—only one person at a time. She was on ventilation; she couldn't speak or understand anything. We, four siblings, went inside her room and met her one by one. By night, we had the news that she was no more.

Now we had her funeral, and as I mentioned in the story, during funeral rituals, it's very essential for a crow to come to eat the favourite food that is kept in memory of the dead in the crematorium. Until the crow doesn't touch the food, no relatives can have it. If it is too long, it is assumed some desire is remaining in the dead person. Then they ask the dog to eat the food; if even the dog refuses, then finally the cow is bought to eat it. If all three crows, dogs, and cows refuse to eat it, then it's a really bad omen. Then some strong, unfulfilled desires remain among the dead.

In my mom's case, all three refused to touch the food. Then there was gossip going on among the relatives who had gathered there. What could be the reason? All suspected it must be the marriage of two of her younger children. My mom was a very quiet and pious lady, so nobody expected this to happen.

The priest then said to each and every member of the family individually, Go and say sorry to her if any of you have hurt her in any manner. All my elder uncles and aunts went and said sorry. Me and my husband said, Mom, don't worry; we will take responsibility for the younger sibling and their marriage. Plz, eat. But still, she refused.

Now only her granddaughter and grandson were remaining. One was 3, and the other was 5. We took them there and asked them to pray. Immediately to our surprise, the crow ate jelabi and rice from the plate.

We failed to realise a simple thing in the ICU: we couldn't take the children along with us. And all she wanted was to see them, and she wanted them near. This is how love is. If you say foolish, it is; if you say blind, it is; if you say it's the universe, it is.

Don't wait to express your love and gratitude after you have a hint of guilt. Do it every day. Teach children to express what's in their hearts. Emojis can't replace words.

MOHAA (GREED)

GREED, IN THE END, FAILS EVEN THE GREEDY

CATHRYN

MONEY ISN'T THE ROOT OF ALL EVIL. GREED IS.

GREED IS THE ATTITUDE THAT'S NEVER QUITE SATISFIED, THAT SAYS, "ALL I WANT IS A LITTLE BIT MORE".

Like me, I think many of you must be wondering that when we perform Satya Narayan puja, or solah (16) somwar vrat, or in that case any puja, we read a story related to that God in front of that God only. Doesn't that seem silly? If God already knows what he has done, and we too have heard it before, then why do we have to repeat it every time we do it? What is its significance? When people were illiterate, how did they perform this puja? when there were no books and they didn't know how to read? I am sure many of you must have encountered this question in your mind, but you didn't know whom to ask or thought it would be morally incorrect to ask such a question, because Granny would surely give an earful.

Stories, fairy tales, and folklore are not only for children. The stories, or, let us say, the narration that we listen to from the pandits who have come to perform the puja at home, remind us of the healthy way to lead our lives. If you listen to these stories, they have some morals to them. Now, coming back to the topic of religion and spirituality, I would say that these stories are like giving you advice in a nutshell. No doubt you religiously did the puja, but the advice and the fruit that you are getting out of this puja is that after you listen to the advice, it's totally up to you to follow it or not. God doesn't force you to follow his advice. That is why his suggestions or advice are given in story form. But as I said, we millennials have forgotten the art of listening. We have lost the patience to hear anyone forget the story. We even want the 3-hour movie to end in one and a half hours. Also, the movie songs are hardly 2 minutes long, while Rafi Saab's songs were around 5 minutes, approx., and it never felt boring listening to him.

Along with the art of listening, I feel the art of storytelling is also going into the dark. I don't know which one comes first. Have we forgotten how to strike good communication, or have we lost the patience to listen to anyone? Please observe, as a psychologist, that when we take a DAPT (draw a person test) to do the analysis of the child and ask the child to draw a picture of a person, interestingly, they will draw eyes, nose, lips, hands, and legs, but many children forget to draw the ears. It shows clearly that we are actually losing the art of communication. Then it may be among the spouse, parents,children, or the entire family and society.

Stories are the best way to communicate. I am saying this because if you want to convey a difficult message, you can tell a story, and the other person will understand what you have to say. That is the way, in the olden days, parents installed moral values in their children and grandchildren. While sleeping, when our subconscious brain is active, that is the best time we can make our children remember anything for a long time. Stories with moral values, or stories of bravery, stories of love and compassion, stories of the great kings and freedom fighters, stories of the rich heritage and culture, stories behind why and how a particular temple was built—when such stories are told to children, surely, they have a positive impact on the psyche of the developing child brain. Stories will not only increase their knowledge, but they will also be able to differentiate well between what is real and what is fantasy. Because of the cartoons they show on television or YouTube, children are getting caught in the web of illusion. They can't differentiate between what is true and what is imaginary because what they see is all true for them. It's a herculean task for parents to present a mirror of reality in front of them and get them back into reality before they go into their own lonely world of imagination.

Talking about stories, as I said, stories are not necessarily events that have happened in the past. They are just formed so that humans take the moral from the story. Here is such a story that I have heard from a famous Varkari from Maharashtra during one of his bhajans and pravachan. He was speaking on the topic of greed, and the story goes somewhat like this:

One day in the Vaikuntha, when Vishnu and Laxmi were sitting and having some conversation, they got into an argument, and Laxmi got angry and said something to Vishnu.

Laxmi: "Lord, do you know, all these people on earth do your bhakti because I am associated with you? I am, and you are. You are nothing without me."

Vishnu: "No, Laxmi, you are wrong, you are what you are, and I am what I am. There can't be any comparison. We both are different individuals.".

Laxmi: "Lord, I can prove what I am saying, you will repent when I leave you and go."

Vishnu:"OK, Laxmi, I will give you 2 months to prove your words, Go ahead and prove me wrong.".

Laxmi: "Yes, I will go on bhoo Loka (earth) and show you how much more important I am to people than you are.".

Vishnu: "Ok, I will accompany you, and see it with my own eyes.".

Both went together on the earth, and as they were passing through, Laxmi saw a procession of people carrying a dead body on road. A lot of people had gathered, and all were crying. Laxmi thought this was a good opportunity, and she said to Vishnu, No need to wait for two months, I will show you my importance right now only.

Laxmi started pouring the rain of currency notes from above. First the people were amazed, shocked, and confused. They looked at each other, and by this time, all had stopped crying and started collecting the currency notes. They had all forgotten about the dead person.

Laxmi, in pride, said, saw how I made people forget the dead and fall for me.

Vishnu replied:" Laxmi, you are not seeing clearly, still, four people are not influenced by you.".

Laxmi said wait, and she showered higher currency notes in front of those four people who were carrying the dead body. At first, they didn't stop themselves from picking it up, but when the rain of currency notes increased, they could not control their temptation. They laid the dead body down and started collecting the notes.

Laxmi started laughing loudly, with pride in her eyes and sarcasm in their voice, and said to Vishu," You see, my value?"

Vishnu smiled and replied with the same tone of sarcasm, "Can't you see the dead body lying there? Your magic hasn't worked there."

Laxmi said, But he is dead, Lord.

Vishnu said, "I AM NOT INSIDE HIM, SO HE DID NOT GET UP TO PICK YOU."

That's why they say, "RAM NAAM SATYA HAI." If I am in the body, you are of value; else this is all just mithya, not satya.

MANN MEIN RAM, KANN KANN MEIN RAM.

HAR SANS ME RAM, NASS NASS MEIN RAM.

DHARTI MEIN RAM, AKASH MEIN RAM.

MANNO TO BHI RAM, NA MANO TOH BHI RAM.

MEERA KI BHAKTI MEIN RAM, RADHA KI PUJA MEIN RAM.

KANHA KI BANSURI MEIN RAM, SHIV KI DAMRU ME RAM.

SHOR MEIN RAM, MANN KE SHANTI ME RAM.

MUJH MEIN RAM TUJHME RAM

FIR KYUN DUNDEE FIRTHE MANDIR ME RAM?

JHAAK KE DEKHO ANDHAR, SAB MIL JAYEGA

KEDAR, VAISHNO, MATHURA, SOM, YE SAB PAYEGA

BAS PYAR SE PUKARO, WOH AA JAYEGA.

JAI SHRI RAM JAI JAI SHRI RAM.

ANUGRAHA

Grace is the face that love wears when it meets imperfection."

Grace is love that has nothing to do with us but everything to do with the love of God for us.

Punarapi jananam punarapi maranam

Punarapi janani jathare shayanam iha sansare khalu dustare

Krupaya pare pahi murare

Repeated Births and repeated deaths

And repeatedly sleeping in the womb of a mother

This ocean of samsara is difficult to cross.

OH GOD, kindly save me and help me to cross.

This shloka is written by Shri Shankaracharya, in which he is humbly requesting God to take him out of this wheel of birth and death. But as we all know, karma does not start with birth or end with death; with a new birth, we have only taken on a new form and a new name, but our karmic account is still the same. We have taken birth, keeping in mind that we are going to clear most of the karmic debts with the help of the spiritual masters by properly planning the situations in our lives and how we are going to work around them. What lessons are we going to learn in this life on earth, and who will be our teachers? Our teachers are nearby. We choose them wisely, like a strict mother or an argumentative husband. The reason is that we do not have these qualities of tolerance in us, and no outsider knows how to learn or which teachers would be good for your learning. If you look at it the other way, they are just actors coming down to teach you something on your demand. When we all go back as souls, there will be only the messy accounts that we have created in human form. Souls cannot hate each other. The drama was only for the earth. If the couple is undergoing a divorce, most of the time it is because of the runanubandhas (karmic connections) they carry from past lives. Do not forget that you have come to teach each other a lesson of love and tolerance, as well as a lesson of trust and peace for your children.

Let us dive a little deeper into the types of karma:

1. Kriyaman karma: Kriyaman karma means an action done on the spur of a moment in the present tense, which instantaneously bears the fruits of the action.

2. Sanchit karma (cumulative karma) means actions have already been taken, but the fruits are not yet ripened to be given. They will remain in balance, and when the time comes, according to the action committed, the corresponding pending ripened fruit will be given.

3. Prarabdha karma: these karmas are out of the sanchit karmas. The fruits are ripened and about to be given. Prarabdha is also known as destiny, fate, and luck.

As souls, we come alone to this school called Earth to learn about life. What about life? EMOTIONS. We are spiritual beings. We have humongous potential, but over time we have forgotten it. The reason is that we do not listen to our own souls. When a soul can travel from heaven to a mother's womb, and survive there in a dark and mushy atmosphere for 9 months without anyone's help, and after death, the soul also does not need direction to know where it must go, then why is it lost and confused in it's entire life?

God himself is so merciful. For his devotees, he has taken so many forms but God can never take away any negative karma from anybody, be he a normal human or God's greatest devotee. All that God can do is shower his grace. I will explain grace in the form of a few real-life stories, among them two out of my life, but before that, I want to explain what grace means.

On the day when the war of Kurukshetra was about to begin, the sides of great warriors were already chosen. Krishna's army was on Duryodhana's side, and Krishna chose to be Arjun's charioteer. Just when the war was about to begin, Arjun got anxious and expressed his nervousness to Krishna. Krishna, being God himself, would have finished the war on Arjun's behalf, or He would have completely avoided the war itself, but as the law of karma goes, "even God cannot make changes in another person's karma.". Instead, God showed his grace in the form of VISHWAROOPA and instead motivated Arjuna to do his karma.

When God decides to bestow grace on his devotees, that elevates the life of the devotee spiritually. And that is what Krishna did by showing grace and motivating Arjuna rather than fighting the war for Arjuna himself. God will help you to think logically while answering the question paper at the school called Earth, but he will not sit to write the exam on your behalf. We get angry at him, sometimes curse him, turn against him, and lose faith in him, but he is the principal of the school, he cannot disown you. He will always have his eyes on you, whether you like it or not.

Let us see in the following stories how God has come down in different forms to his devotees.

As I said, these stories are not from any written source; two of the stories we are hearing are from our ancestors only, and another is a famous folk tale; a famous Marathi movie is also made on it. There are many versions of the story. But I chose to write what was told by an old grandmother near my house from Konkan.

Thamb Laxmi kunku lavte

(Do not leave Laxmi; let me apply kumkum on your forehead.)

There is a small village in Konkan. Konkan was a beautiful place with clean waters, cashew trees, mango trees, coconut trees, and banana trees. Everything was beautiful except the landlord, who exploited the people around him. A few generations ago, these landlords were the most revered families in the Konkan area, not only because of their ancestors, who were good rulers and took care of the villages, but also because they had a boon from God. And that boon was Swayambhoo Laxmi paduka (Laxmi footprints). Maa had come in the dream of one of the ancestors and had told him, Vilasrao, I am incredibly happy with how sincerely you deal with your farmers. They are happy. If I go to some poor house, he will spend all the money on his luxuries, but if I stay in your safe, I am sure you will do justice to all, and I will be in your house for generations. So, it is my promise that till my Puja is done here and your coming generations work with honesty, I will always be in this house. Your house will never fall short of anything. But after a few generations, things changed. Greed started getting into the mind of the great great grand-son of Vilas Rao. Out of two conditions, only one was being fulfilled, and that was Devi's Puja, performed by Vilas Rao's great-great granddaughter-in-law Bhagy.

(*Laxmi maa is patal vasini. She stays in Patal. How do we know this? Gold comes from under the earth. Food grows under the earth. Same with gems, diamonds or anything precious, even water).

Because of greed, the landlord was taxing the farmers. He was intoxicated the entire day, indulging in adultery. He did everything that he should not have done. Maa came in dreams of Bhagya twice to make her aware of her husband's bad habits, but it was in vain. Bhagya started getting anxious, she knew something worse was going to happen, and then suddenly one evening there was a lady at the door wearing a green sari, and green bangles. Very divine looking. Bhagya was mesmerised. Bhagya said, “Please come inside and sit; do not stand out.” The lady said, "No, I have come to bid goodbye.".

Something struck Bhagya; she went running inside and saw there were no footprints of Laxmi. She understood that Laxmi was leaving her house now. But somehow, Bhagya did not want that to happen. She came smiling and said "Thamb Laxmi kunku lavte" with tears in her eyes and went inside to get the kumkum.

Now it becomes necessary to know why Bhagya asks Laxmi to wait.

In the Hindu religion, haldi and kumkum are held remarkably high in respect. No marriage ceremony or any pooja ceremony is complete without the groom applying kumkum to the bride's forehead. Well, in the centre between our eyebrows, there is a chakra known as the third eye chakra, or agya chakra. We apply turmeric there, as it has antiseptic qualities, and kumkum to activate the third eye chakra. But this is the spiritual reason. After marriage, women apply kumkum to each other during ceremonies and pujas with the sense that, "May your husband have a long and prosperous life, so do you ". Those were patriarchal days, so if men in the house were happy, women were happy. And it was considered a huge disrespect if haldi kumkum was not applied to married women when the guests were about to leave the house. So, Laxmi had to wait, but to her surprise, Bhagya did not come back with kumkum. She ran towards the backyard and jumped in the well so that Laxmi would wait there in her house as" sthir laxmi " forever, thinking Bhagya would come back with Kumkum.

Laxmi had to stay back, without choice. This house is still present in Kokan. But people say that now Laxmi has left the house as the generation has come to an end.

Humans don't realise how important the grace of God is. So many times I have heard people complain after a massive accident that God was unfair to them .How could God do this to me? I feel like saying, foolish man, you are standing here and abusing God because of his grace. What if you had a fatal accident and lost the family, or if someone else would be hurt because of you? Isn't it God's grace that whatever little happens can be repaired? And it could be completely your fault; why are you even blaming God? Do you ever thank him when you reach home safely? Isn't that grace? What if a drunk fellow commits an accident and it's not your fault.

TWIST OF DESTINY

Life always gives us the exact teacher.

We need it at every moment.

This includes every mosquito.

Every misfortune. Every red light,

Every traffic jam,

Every obnoxious supervisor,

Every illness, every loss,

Every moment of joy or depression,

Every addiction,

Every piece of garbage, every breath.

Every moment is the GURU.

Charlotte Joko Beck

Before a soul decides to take birth, it has to decide what lessons it will come down on earth to learn. Accordingly, the soul will select its parents. Because parents are closest to us, parents are able to be the best teachers for the soul. So it is seen that many souls opt for one strict parent with whom they don't get along, and then when they take birth, they forget about the choices they made and start the quarrel, wherein they lose the chance of learning the lesson and completing the task on earth.

The soul, with the help of soul guides and guardian angels, not only gets the chance to choose the parents but also the life situations. The soul and the soul guide plan life beforehand, looking into what lessons the soul still needs to learn. It takes numerous births to master one lesson. That's because when we give birth, we take our lives so casually that we get carried away with the way we are not supposed to live. Temptations are at every nook and cranny of our way on earth, and that is what is explained in Bhagavad Gita as MAYA. MAYA is nothing complex; let us take, for example, that if a person knows that he has borderline diabetes and giving up sugar is the wisest thing he can do right now, but the web (Jaal) of Maya is so strong on him that he will convince himself that he can give up anything but sugar. But here, the question is not about giving up sugar; you had borderline diabetes, and you were tested for your willpower. You are destined to get diabetes if you continue to eat sugar and carbohydrates, but God has also given you the choice of free will. With that free will, do you have that much willpower and self-control to give up sugar? So, this is Maya and the concept of destiny and free will.

So as I said, the guardian angels help us to decide the blueprint of life; they help us select the challenges and lessons to learn and finish with the fruits of some of the karma. These guardian angels are present with us throughout our lives to guide us. The gut instinct that we have says that these angels are speaking to us.

This is the story of Krishna Patil, who lives in Dahanu in the Palghar district of Maharashtra. Dahanu is a coastal town 100 kilometres north of Mumbai. Krishna came from an upper-middle-class family. He had nothing major to complain about. Almost all his wishes were fulfilled by his parents. His mother was an excellent cook. She cooked whatever Krishna wanted to eat. Krishna's father was a diploma electrical engineer and did business as an electrical contractor for the Government Electricity Department. His only unfulfilled desire was that he couldn't complete a degree in engineering. Krishna's father was a farmer and was very poor. He couldn't even afford to send his children to school. However, Krishna's father managed to complete his matriculation from a government school and borrowed money from a money lender to complete his diploma in engineering. After that, he had to do jobs to pay the lender's money back. He had struggled and worked very hard to reach the financial position that he has today. His only wish was that Krishna should get a degree in electrical engineering and continue his business.

Krishna was a bright student. He passed his 10th standard exam with distinction. However, in 12th grade, he became wayward because of his friends. He lost interest in his studies and started bunking school to go and watch movies with his friends. However, he managed to pass the 12th standard with minimum marks. His father was furious. He had expected him to score good marks and secure admission to a good engineering college. But his father somehow managed to secure admission to a reputed engineering college in Bangalore. Krishna joined the college in Bangalore but was not interested in engineering from day one. He didn't wish to do engineering but feared his father, so he couldn't say anything. He also didn't like the hostel in which he was staying. He felt trapped and unhappy in his situation.

Two toilets and two bathrooms were shared by fifty students. So, Krishna only bathed on Sundays because other students would get up late. He didn't even have time for breakfast. He would get ready by 7:50 in the morning and have to run to college, which started at 8 o'clock. He didn't understand anything that was taught in college, so he kept staring out the window. His professors scolded him, but that didn't deter him from staring out of the window. So finally, the professors gave up and said, Do whatever you want. He didn't even like the college mess food. It was not as tasty as what his mother would cook. He missed his mother's food a lot. His health started to get worse. He was also mentally depressed.

Finally, after completing the first semester, he came back home and told his parents that he couldn't continue his engineering course because he could understand nothing. He had no interest in physics, mathematics, or chemistry. His parents were extremely disappointed. But Krishna cried for two days to allow him to leave engineering. Finally, after consulting a few astrologers, they agreed. The astrologers told his parents to allow Krishna to study anything he wanted; otherwise, he wouldn't study at all.

Krishna told his parents that he wanted to do a Bachelor of Computer Application course.

His parents were initially hesitant, but eventually agreed to support his decision. Krishna was thrilled to finally pursue a subject he was passionate about and felt confident in. Krishna's mother had a cousin's brother in Dharwad. Dharwad was well known for its colleges and good education at that time. Krishna's father contacted Krishna's mother's cousin for admission. He said that admissions are open for the course and asked to send Krishna immediately.

So, Krishna took a bus from Mumbai to Dharwad and reached Dharwad early in the morning. Now here comes the twist. His maternal uncle had a very beautiful elder daughter, pallavi. She was dusky but had an extremely beautiful smile, beautiful eyes, and a voice. She was wearing a blue dress when she came out in the living room to meet Krishna. Both eyes meet and the cupid strikes. Krishna fell in love with her at first sight. The first time he saw her, her eyes were sparkling like diamonds. It was destined for them to meet and fall in love. Krishna stayed there for three days. Filled out all the forms. But on the fourth day, Krishna's father called him and said he had secured admission for him to a reputed college in Pune. He had by this time thought that he would study in Dharwad and spend time with pallavi. But he had to leave for Pune. Krishna also liked pallavli's mother a lot. She was very caring and a good cook, just like his mother. She gave him a steel tiffin with food while Krishna was leaving their home. This, too, won Krishna's heart.

Krishna joined the college in Pune for a BCA course. Initially, he found it difficult to adjust. But he had good roommates, so slowly he started to adjust. Days passed. He missed Pallavi a lot. Finally, he managed to gather the courage to propose to Pallavi after exchanging a few emails. Both eagerly waited for each other's emails. Mobile phones were very expensive at the time, so students couldn't afford them. Pallavi also expressed his love for him on Valentine's Day. Krishna waited for her phone call on a landline in his paying guest owner's home. He waited till 6 o'clock in the evening for the call. Then he started crying. So, his friend forced him to go to a phone booth and call Pallavi at her home. He somehow mustered the courage and called her. Pallavi picked up the phone. She told him that he had been trying to call him since afternoon, but Krishna's landline phone was giving a busy tone. She even changed many booths, but to no avail. Krishna felt happy. She didn't say she loved him on the phone, as her mother was also present, but she told him she had emailed him. So, Krishna ran out of the phone booth and went into a cybercafé. The Internet was not widely available at that time, so there were cyber cafes with computers and Internet access. He opened his email inbox, and there was an email from her saying she loved him. They used to chat from cyber cafes, as phone calls were also very expensive during those days. Occasionally, they called each other. Somehow, the parents of both Krishna and Pallavi came to know about their affair. Pallavi's parents liked Krishna but were not very sure of Krishna's parents. They thought Krishna's parents wouldn't agree to marriage. And that was true. Krishna's parents wanted to marry him into a rich and influential family. But Krishna was adamant. So, after Krishna completed his MBA in Mumbai, Pallavi's father came with the marriage proposal at Krishna's home.

Krishna's parents had no choice but to accept it, even when they didn't want to.

So finally, Krishna and pallavi got married. Krishna was very happy after marriage, but pallavi wasn't. Krishna's mother always said mean things to her. Krishna's sister, who had separated from his husband, lived there. Even though she was very mean to her, They would even scold her if she talked over the phone with her parents. Pallavi used to cry the whole night. She was highly educated. She had a degree in engineering. She wanted to do a job. She finally managed to secure a job at a manufacturing company. But things became worse after that. Krishna and pallavi started to fight because his mother gave her a very hard time. Finally, Krishna decided to live separately from his parents. Initially, they agreed somehow, but the day before he was supposed to leave, his father disagreed and told him not to leave. Financially, Krishna was dependent on his father, as he worked in his father's business. This angered Krishna a lot, and he decided to leave home at night without telling anyone and go to Pune and start a new life.

They wrote a letter to his parents and left home at midnight. They went to Pune and lived in Krishna's friend's home for three days. Krishna's parents searched for them, as Krishna didn't tell them where he was going. Finally, they came to know him and visited him in Pune. They said they were sorry and urged him to come back, but Krishna was adamant. He didn't go back. Krishna's friend, whom he trusted a lot, told him to vacate his home after three days. This broke Krishna's heart. Krishna didn't have enough money to rent a flat in Pune, so Pallavi had to go to Dharwad, and Krishna stayed with his other bachelor friends. He didn't have money to buy a bed, so he borrowed a straw mattress (Chattai) from his friend and slept on it. He felt as if a prince had suddenly become dirt poor. He had never experienced what he was experiencing.

He spent days searching for a job. At night, his legs ache due to walking. He didn't have money to rent an auto rickshaw or cab, so he had to go on foot for interviews. They didn't go everywhere, so many times he had to walk a few kilometres to reach the interviews. But he was rejected everywhere. He didn't even have money to eat two times a day. So, he ate vada pav in the afternoon and had dinner at night.

After a month, Pallavi told Krishna to rent a flat in Pune, as she didn't want to stay at her father's home anymore. So somehow, Krishna managed to rent a flat. They bought cotton mattresses and slept on the ground. After six months, Krishna managed to get a job at a reputed company with decent pay. Pallavi also started earning money by teaching at an engineering college. They were satisfied and happy. Pallavi was pregnant at that time. But tragedy struck them again. After six months of pregnancy, it was found in sonography that their baby had many disabilities. Doctors advised abortion. If born, the baby will have mental as well as physical disabilities. So, the baby was aborted. It was a girl. Krishna wanted a baby girl, but it was not in his destiny. Pallavi became pregnant again but a few months later, the same thing happened. The baby was aborted again. Both were grief-stricken but couldn't do anything in front of destiny. After three years, Krishna was double promoted. He was very good at work. His seniors were very happy with his work. But Krishna thought he was paid very little for the job he did. Others had left the company and joined another company and had gotten a good raise. Juniors who joined later had a higher salary than Krishna. So, Krishna decided to look for another company. He went to a company for an interview but was rejected. Krishna's bad luck was far from over. His seniors got wind of this, and he was again demoted. His team was broken and divided, and he was no longer a team leader. This depressed Krishna a lot. He was no longer interested in work. He went into depression and had anxiety. He finally resigned from the company. Krishna's father told him to come back. He accepted his father's offer and wanted to go back. But after a few months, he had to give in and come to Dahanu. However, they live separately from Krishna's parents in a flat.

Pallavi got pregnant two more times, but the same fate struck them. Finally, they succeeded a fifth time and had a baby boy. Krishna was elated and extremely happy after a very long time.

From then on, only good luck followed him. He opened his own business independently of his father and was very successful. His father, who thought his son was good for nothing, was finally proud of him. Finally, after so many twists in Krishna's destiny and so much struggle, his destiny smiled at him. And it must be said that Pallavi was the reason for his success in business. She supported him emotionally as well as in decision-making.

The lesson that Krishna had to learn was to be humble and to have patience. Maybe he will master them in this lifetime.

VERMILLION: THE COLOUR OF LOVE AND DEVOTION.

The moment I realize God lives in the temple of every human body, the moment I stand in reverence before every human being and see God in God in him- that moment I am free from bondages, everyone, everything that binds vanishes, and I am free.

Does truth exist without evidence?

The symbolism of offering water to a beloved deity in relation to the purity and serenity of true love. Delving deeper into the theme of divine intervention bringing two souls together in moments of true love.

Suprabhat, Mr. and Mrs. Banerjee, may I look at your bookings, please?

This was the sweet voice of a young girl around 37 years old, standing across the reception desk of a 5-star Hotel and guiding the guests through the formalities of the check-in. She had the sweetest voice and the smile that even Madhubala and Madhuri Dixit would acknowledge, but who am I talking about?

I am talking about Aarashi, well Ms. S.K. Aarashi, who is basically from Tamil Nadu, completed her Hotel Management course which her strict and orthodox parents never wanted her to do, but she went against their wishes and completed it. She did another thing that her parents had warned her not to do, and she fell in love with a non-Tamilian, who was not even of her same caste.

That was the biggest sin she had committed. Now she had no place in their house as well as in their hearts.

Aarashi had to pack her stuff and move in with her boyfriend. A few days of her live-in relationship with her boyfriend went well. The guy she had moved in with had also studied hotel management with her and was an expert in bartending. He was a handsome-looking guy. His colleagues teased him saying that chicks come for an extra drink just to flirt with him.

Obviously, Aarashi did not like his flirtatious behavior when she heard about him from their common friends, but she knew she was deeply in love with Rahul Singh, her boyfriend. She mustered her strength one day and asked him: Rahul, shall we get married? We have been living together for almost a year now; wouldn't it be nice if we started a family?

Rahul was lying down on the sofa, playing a mobile game, when he suddenly looked up at her in her eyes, stared for a minute, and said, sit, sit down there on the floor, "do you know what you are talking about? You are staying here because I had mercy on you. Don't think I am your boyfriend, and you are my only girlfriend.

Aarashi, you have a front desk job, so you leave the house early. Your working hours are opposite to mine. Do you even know what happens here when you leave the flat? Get the things straight in your head. I helped you just as a homeless person; don't expect anything more from me.

Listening to this, Aarashi almost collapsed crying. She was asking Krishna "Are you happy now seeing me in this condition"? She was a devotee of "Guruvayur Krishna".(The temple, dedicated to lord vishnu and the young form of lord krishna, is also known as Guruvayur Sree Krishna Temple. There is a most famous legend attached to the temple. Legend has it that Krishna set his charioteer.Udhava, to save Vishnu idol from being worshipped by him in Dwaraka. Udava seeked the help of Lord Vayu and took the statue away and installed it at Guruvayur) He was like a childhood friend to her, although she had never been there as it was in neighboring states but something about Him always attracted her.

She got up, went into the room, and sat in front of the Krishna statue and said, "Happy *alla*"? (Happy now) what do you get by doing all this to me? I was in less trouble already and you pushed me into another one. Tell me now, where I go, what I should do, I know, you won't tell me anything, you can only smile at my misery.

She packed her stuff from Rahul Singh's house and was thinking about what to do next, but nothing, no idea, was coming up. Finally, she managed to keep the luggage at her friend's flat and reported to the job right on time. Today her smile was not as charming as always and that really made the atmosphere dull.

You can replace 100 lamps, 1000 roses, or even the finest of the fragrances but some smiles are irreplaceable. Looking at her face, HR called Aarashi into the office and asked her why she was dull today. If she was not well, maybe she could take leave. Aarashi said," No ma'am I am ok," Aarashi hesitated for a while but later mustered courage and asked, "Ma'am can I get a transfer to our hotels anywhere in India."

HR got worried and asked, "Is anyone harassing you here, it's against the rules, please bring it to my notice, and I will take care of it."

Arashi said "No ma'am, please, I want to go far away from this place. Please help me madam this time. I will be grateful."

As soon as Aarashi came out of the HR office the first thing she did was write an email to the head office and started waiting for the reply. By evening she had received a reply to the email saying she could opt for transfer to the Kolkata hotel branch. Arashi didn't seem very happy at first.

She thought to herself where Coimbatore is and where is Kolkata? I don't even know anyone there. Also, it's so far. Then she took a deep breath and talked to herself calmly, "Look Aarashi, why does distance matter to you now?

"Distance between the hearts decides true emotions of relationships; not the kilometers," also, why do you want to know anyone? You are going there for a job, to start new; slowly, you will start getting to know people. And anyways you are running away from people and situations here. Why are you thinking so much? Maybe you will " find yourself " in the unknown people there.

What help have you got till today? From now on build your own tribe of people; take the offer, Aarashi remembers Bengal is the land of Maa Kali and says I am a warrior, that is why I am given the offer of Kolkata.

She accepted the offer.

Finally, she was welcomed in "The Pride Palace, Kolkata" by a small team, as a welcome gesture. She loved it. She finished her joining formalities and started with her job at the front desk immediately. The problem here was that she was asked to learn Bengali before she joined, as it was a requirement of the post.

Aarashi being a hard-working girl also learned Bengali very fast, there used to be no mistakes technically but the accent "Imagine a Tamil girl speaking Bengali". (it sounded extremely sweet)

It wasn't funny, but it was sort of a mismatch. But all her colleagues never discouraged her and always spoke to her in Bengali so that her language got more refined. Gradually, she started exploring the city. She found it a little crowded though. She started loving those yellow taxis and Howrah Bridge.

She usually did not go out with friends drinking or nights out. Watch some Tamil or Malayalam movies on Netflix. She was a diehard fan of Vijay Sethupathi. She also loved listening to old Hindi songs. She had started forgetting the past and enjoying her new life of freedom.

On holidays when there were no good movies to watch on Netflix, she would hop into a yellow taxi and drive to the Ganga ghat, the exact ghat from where the Howrah bridge is visible. She would see people boating in water, some eating *bhelpuri,* but she would sit there till sunset with earphones in her ears, listening to Kishore Kumar's "*Kiska rasta dekhe, ye dil, ye saudai...*" in a loop.

It was her go-to song when she felt sad. After mustering the courage, she used to tell herself, you are strong Aarashi, she would take a long sigh and head back to her flat in a yellow taxi. That evening she came home, changed into comfortable clothes, and lay on the sofa scrolling Facebook.

She found nothing interesting there either. She went on scrolling, then she switched to Instagram and the same scrolling, found only ads, ads, and more ads, she felt Facebook was better so she came back to Facebook, where while scrolling she paused for a second to read:

"You will not enter paradise until you have faith. And you will not complete your faith until you love one another" – Prophet Muhammad.

She smiled at the quote and remembered the fool she was to have loved Rahul Singh. She had gone beyond the heartbreak for sure as she did not feel like crying.

As she scrolled further, she came across a page which she was a member of, the Facebook page name was, "True Soulmates'. And suddenly Aarashi remembered that after her heartbreak with Rahul, she was searching for a true soul mate and so she joined the group.

Something lit up in her mind, as she saw someone by the name of Roy Deb had put on a post " In need of a true soul mate. Hope I will find one here". Aarashi laughed at the post first and said who the fxxx writes such things here. Then immediately she went to check the comments in the comments box.

She found that 90% of the comments were mean and nasty, and only a few were like awwwww, bless you, may you find your true soul mate etc. Aarashi felt bad for the author of the post, she thought that some 17-18-year-old boy who didn't even know what soulmate is, was writing this and the poor thing was getting nasty comments back.

She immediately DM (directly messaged) Roy Deb, she didn't even know who he was, as there was no display picture of his face. Immediately the reply came - Hi!

Aarashi: Did you write a post on true soulmates?

RD: Yes

Aarashi: Ohh, would you mind taking it down, please.

RD: Why? What happened?

Aarashi: See, beta you are hardly a teenager, if you read such nasty comments, it will harm your studies, and by the way what is your name and where do you stay?

RD: Wait ma'am, you breathe first, my name is Deb Roy, but on Facebook, it is Roy Deb. I am from Kolkata and I am not a 17-year-old teenager, I am a 32-year-old chap. Two minutes passed and there was no message from Aarashi.

RD: Hello ma'am.... hello

Aarashi: I am so sorry, Sir. I am very sorry. I didn't mean to interfere, but soulmates are not found this way on the internet, and you posted that, people were mean to you, so I interfered.

RD: It's ok, thank you so much for your concern, and above all thinking brains is that of a 17-year-old, what a compliment. I didn't get your name ma'am.

Aarashi: S.K Aarashi.

RD: Non-Bengali

Aarashi: Yep, Tamilian.

RD: OK then ma'am, anyways thanks.

Aarashi: Wait, wait, I wanted to ask you something? What is that picture you have put in your DP?

RD: Oh, that, (RD smiles) It's a long story (it was a picture of a silver bangle and a *nathani* (nose ring), but very antique)

Aarashi: 99XXXXX999 This is my number; you can call this number and tell me that long story.

Deb was shocked for a moment, how could a girl directly give her number? That too to hear about the display picture, was something fishy?

He started thinking in his mind but thought of giving her a call later and then there was a message from the other side saying, "You know Debji it's been 20 years or more since nobody has told me a story only my ammo (my granny) would tell me a story when she used to oil my hair, so that I don't move and listen with whole concentration, but she usually told me stories about Ramayana or Mahabharata but never about women goddesses. Please tell me, I would like to hear it."

Now Deb is in fix. Who was Deb? Deb Roy is a 32-year-old professional working in an MNC, in Kolkata. He earned well, he was intelligent, and he had a handsome package. He was a good-looking guy. A boy you can introduce your mother to, without feeling awkward, he didn't drink, and yes, he smoked, but not a chain smoker. when everything was so good then what was the desperation of that post of finding a true soulmate on the internet?

There were several reasons, one is that he had lost his father last year and his mother was making life difficult for him. She used to come up with a new excuse for not cooking, saying she was not feeling well, so Deb had to cook, do all the household chores, take her to the doctor, and then to the office. He tried many alternatives.

Such as keeping the maid but his mom treated her so badly that she ran in a day, she was very harsh with her words, complaining and complaining and only complaining. Ordering food from Zomato or Swiggy, she said she hates eating outside food, and that food only made her ill. The idea of keeping a 24-hour nurse, she lamented that bringing a nurse home would take away all her deposited money.

Deb, a fun-loving guy, had turned into a lonely soul. He used to come from work, see if Mother had prepared anything, or just go out and get egg rolls for both, eat, and go in the bedroom and log into Facebook. Facebook has become his second home now. He hadn't even thought of falling into a relationship because he was a mess, his emotions were a mess, his house was a mess, his family was a mess and his whole life was a mess.

Aarashi: Deb, Debji are you there?

Deb: Ha yes

Aarashi: So, will you tell me the story?

Deb: Over the call?

Aarashi: Yes, why not, now is a good time, oh, sorry I didn't ask if you are free or not? I said because I was free.

Deb: Ok then Aarashi ma'am can I call on your cell, at home your husband would mind it's almost 9:15 PM.

Aarashi laughed and said, "No you can call, I am eagerly waiting."

Aarashi went inside to grab a bottle of water and when she returned her cell was already vibrating on the table, the true caller flashing the name DEBADEY ROY. She immediately picked up the phone and said hello in such a sweet voice that Deb felt his ears were made to hear this voice only. Till today, whatever he had heard is totally noise.

He said, "Hi Aarashi", then there was a long pause, no one was saying anything, sort of an awkward movement, who would break the ice first?

Finally, Aarashi breaks the silence and asks why you put the DP (display photo) of a bangle and *nath* (nose ring)? That is so unique. Usually, no boy puts it? looking at it, I thought you were a minor.

Deb said these two things have a very special place in my heart. I usually don't care what people think. I do what I think is right to do.

Arashi said, "Yes that is true now start the story.

Deb started narrating the story saying, "Nearly 600 years ago, a Brahmin family migrated from a village to a village in a Hooghly district. The headman of the family was Goddess Kali's devotee. He performed her prayers and puja daily. He died of old age. He had a daughter who was also Goddess Kali's devotee, but during those days women did not perform puja and rituals openly.

After her father's death, this daughter was married off to a man from the same village. That man (her husband) survived for a few years, and he too died. But this girl had no trace of sadness or tears in her eyes upon the death of her husband.

Rather, when the husband's dead body was kept at the front door, she went inside the room wearing bangles, *nath*, put *kumkum, and alta* on her hands and legs, wore a red and white sari and wore a *shakha-pola* (red and white bangles) and came out. Everybody was shocked. People thought she had gone insane.

But she announced loudly that none would touch her. She lifted an earthen pot filled with Ganga water and asked people to carry the body of her husband behind her. She stopped at a particular spot and asked that the cremation could be done there. The priest said as you two have no children, then you only must light the fire. She did so then after performing one last salutation to her husband she jumped into the fire.

All were in shock. So was Aarashi. She said '*Aiyoo papa...*'

Deb said, wait, wait, the story is not over yet. After a few days, she came into the dreams of some of her family members and said, you all failed to recognize me. I am still eager to be with the family. She said to go to the place where the pyre was lit there you will find my bangle and *Nath,* bring it home, I will never leave your side. From the next year on, a Durga Puja pandal was set up there using that bangle and nose ring. This is a 600-year-old story.

Aarashi: gasped devre! Means - oh god.

Deb: Happy?

Aarashi: Very happy. Thank you so much, next time when I want to hear a story, I will surely call you, ok?

Deb: Only said hmmm

Aarashi: Good night.

Deb: Good night.

Deb went to bed thinking what this is all about? Who is this girl? She seems from a good house. Are such souls walking the earth even today? Or maybe I am overthinking. He brushed the thoughts of Aarashi aside and went to bed.

There Aarashi was so impressed with the story that she realized more than four months had passed for her here in Kolkata and not even once had she visited the Dakshineswar mother Kali temple. She felt guilty but was very happy like a little girl inside after listening to the story that night. She slept very peacefully just like on her grandmother's lap.

The next morning as soon as she opened her eyes, yawned, took her cell, and dropped a good morning message to Deb immediately she received a message "Suprabhat".

She smiled to herself and replied "Suprabhat Deb Babu" The chat was done for the day.

The next morning again, Aarashi dropped the message "Suprabhat Deb Babu ' and immediately replied, "Suprabhat." These went on for 5 days then on Friday after Suprabhat Aarashi wrote in chat that Debji you remember now, today is the story day...turning you into my granny now?

Both sent each other LOL messages. Then Aarashi asked Deb to call her for a second, and he said yes...

Aarashi: Hello Deb

Deb: Hello

Aarashi: Can we meet today and then you tell me a story?

Deb: Ok that's fine with me.

Aarashi: OK then after office at 6.

Deb: Where?

Aarashi: Ganga ghat

Deb: Ganga-ghat, not Cafe Coffee Day?

Aarashi: No, Ganga ghat from where Howrah Bridge is visible.

Deb: OK fine, shall I come to pick you up?

Aarashi: No Deb, I will come by yellow taxi, be there by 6:30PM, ok.

Both smiled and started looking forward to 6:00PM.

This was the first time that they were going to meet each other. She was wearing her office sari only, draped to perfection, and properly done make-up, and her beautiful smile made her look divine, just like her name Aarashi. She came out of the hotel, caught the yellow taxi, and was led directly to the Ganga ghat.

Deb on that day was celebrating a fun Friday in the office. So, he was in his jeans and a white T-shirt. Before leaving the office, he went to the washroom to check if his hair was proper. He wore perfume twice and then he left for Ganga-ghat. Deb was handsome-looking, intelligent, lonely, arrogant, and knowledgeable.

Aarashi reached early and sitting on the ghat she was watching the boats dancing on the waves. Within some time, Deb came there, she got up from the place and shook hands with Deb. She introduced herself as Aarashi and he said I am Deb, the first few minutes they introduced themselves. Aarashi told everything about her family, her college, her failed love, and her new journey in Kolkata, she trusted Deb at the first instant.

Deb reciprocated by telling her all his worries and tensions and about his overacting mother. After this dense conversation, there was a long pause, both staring at the dance of the water, the boats, and the open sky.

Deb looked at his watch and said Aarashi , it's late, we should get going.

Arashi said, but you didn't narrate the story today?

Deb said oh story, we can meet again tomorrow if you are free. I will tell you a very fine story. I promise.

Aarashi agreed to meet the next day.

One thing Deb observed was that Aarashi was much older than him. He was 32 and she was 37, but she was very bubbly, she smiled at every sentence she spoke, she really had a divine smile. She was a little dusky but with kohl, her eyes looked bolder and more beautiful.

The most outstanding feature was her little *bindi* (a decorative mark worn in the middle of her forehead) she wore in between her eyebrows to enhance that beautiful white smile. Deb went thinking home about her, he had fallen for her, surely.

Aarashi also liked him, but she had developed a commitment phobia, she was not over with Rahul yet, and she had sensed that Deb is much gentler than Rahul; above all Deb knows how to treat women well.

She had observed Deb very minutely in the first meeting only. small things like opening the taxi door for her when Bhel-puri came, offering her first, he cleaned the floor first before she sat, while getting up, he held her purse and then gave her a hand to get up. She admired all the things. Rahul had never done this to her.

The next day they went for lunch, had a tasty lunch in a quiet place, and exchanged little talks, giggles, little laughs, likes and dislikes. Likes and dislikes were almost the same, but they would not stop fighting over who is best Kishore Kumar or Mohammed Rafi.

When the sun went down a little, Deb and Aarashi went to Ganga Ghat. This was story time. This time she agreed to hop on his bike. They both looked good together when they arrived at the ghat. As usual, he cleaned the place for her to sit and he sat next to her.

For a long time, there was a pause, then Aarashi got irritated and said:" Deb from yesterday You are making me wait for the story"

Deb said "Arey pagli" I was thinking shall I tell you the story of Gopal or Goddess Kali?

Aarashi jumped in excitement Krishna, Krishna, please I love him very much, but he doesn't seem to love me back I don't know why? He never comes when I call.

Deb smiled and started with the story, "There was a small village in Odisha, where a rich landlord lived with his wife and daughter. He had huge lands and everything to be contented about in life, he was living a happy life, then one day a poor boy on a thunderous night took shelter near his house, the next day the owner found out about this orphan boy, his heart melted for him and told his wife that from today this boy will stay with us only, no need to search for his parents.

The girl and the boy played together. They were happy with each other so the owner one day announced that when these two reached their marriage age I would get them married.

Years went by, and when they turned 21, one day he came to the landlord and said, see I have become a marriageable age now, give your daughter's hand into mine. We will live happily. The landlord started laughing and said, I never utter such words ever, his wife also denied it out of fear.

The boy started crying and said I know there was one *Sakshi* (witness) when you said this. The landlord said, oh ok, is it? Mocking him, said go, go and get him, if he gives the witness, I will give my daughter hand in your hand.

The boy went crying from there, on foot towards Mathura, to get Krishna as his *Sakshi*. He always believed in Krishna and thought he would come to give *Sakshi*, so he was walking westwards from Odisha towards Uttar Pradesh. He rested wherever he found a good shade under a tree during the day and at night found a temple to sleep in.

So, one night it happened that he had a dream that Krishna was standing in front of him and asking him "Why are you walking so far to meet me?"

The boy replied, "My beloved Krishna, my landlord had promised his daughter's hand to me, and now he is changing his words. Lord, you were the witness. I know you are omnipresent; I know you have heard it; I want you to come with me to Odisha and tell my landlord to marry me to his daughter.

Krishna smiled, "Ok but I have one condition."

The boy asked, "What is it?"

Krishna said, "Look, you will walk in front, and I will follow you."

The boy immediately raised his doubt" How will I know you are following me?"

Krishna said, "You will hear my anklets ringing, but the moment you turn back, I will turn into the stone then and there only", do you agree with the deal"?

The boy jumped on his feet, realized it wasn't a dream in the first place, and started walking back towards Odisha, as the boy put his first foot on the ground and lifted the other one to put down, he heard the anklets of Krishna ringing with such a melodious sound.

The music of the anklets was so mesmerizing that the boy forgot when they almost reached the boundaries of Odisha. Odisha was Orissa then and was blessed with the side boundaries of the Bay of Bengal, so as they landed on the coastal line, Krishna's *ghungroo* (anklets) stopped making any sound, the boy walked a little farther thinking Krishna must be tired and may be standing on the sand to rest his leg.

Quite a while went by, still, the anklets were not ringing, then finally the boy lost his patience and looked back and found that Krishna was not even a foot away from him, but now he had turned into a statue of stone, but the anklets were still silver.

Then he went to the village running and said see Gopal has come to give *Sakshi*, he called all the villagers, and to everyone's surprise, there really was a statue of a Gopal standing there. The landlord believed that little boy and said, did you really bring the Gopal to give

Sakshi. The landlord bowed down to Gopal and got the boy and his daughter married.

Now there is a temple in Odisha nearly 40 km from Puri, it is known as the "*Sakshi* Gopal" temple.

Then Deb looked at Aarashi and gave a broad smile and while listening to the story, Aarashi just side-hugged Deb and said, "This is one of the best stories I have ever heard".

Deb asked if she wanted to go there and she danced and said yes, yes. So, is the plan fixed for next week?

"Sure", Aarashi said.

Deb dropped Aarashi off at her flat. She was opening the door when a WhatsApp message flashed on her cell, the name was saved as a "storyteller" `, and it said, "My dear listener, this storyteller has millions of stories to tell you. This Saturday or once-a-week thing will not work if you want to listen to many more such stories.

So, this storyteller came up with an idea, "why not miss the listener becoming the better half of Mr. Storyteller, what could be a better combination other than pepper and salt and Tamil and Bengali.

Aarashi, I love you and I want to marry you.

His next message was, look Aarashi, these are my feelings which I expressed from my side. "I am not forcing you for anything you say yes or no, I will still be your "official storyteller" You can't fire me and the plan for Puri next week is ON irrespective of your answer.

Aarashi read the message and went to the balcony, she was all blushing, reading the message as she stood on the balcony and saw that Deb was still waiting for her to come in the balcony and say yes, she did come she smiled and waved bye-bye he sent a flying kiss towards her.

The next morning as a habit, Aarashi picked up her cell and saw the message from the storyteller as "Suprabhat Mrs. Roy". She smiled and put the pillow on her face.

She replied, "Suprabhat Mr. Roy."

This was un-conversational love going on between the two, which he had already expressed but Aarashi was afraid of any commitment because of previous experience. Both their eyes, their body language, their expressions everything showed how much they loved each other.

Finally, on Saturday they started by train from Howrah to Puri. They got down at Puri and took the *darshan* of the beautiful Jagannath temple. She was mesmerized seeing her Krishna from so nearby. All the pundits over there treated them as a newlywed couple.

As Aarashi was wearing a sari she was looking stunning. In Puri, they entered the Rukmini Mata temple and the priest said "*Dono Jodi se namaskar karo*" (both do salutation together) and he asked him to put *kumkum* on her forehead, she was reluctant, but that strict pandit ji said today's children because of selfies don't want to spoil their makeup.

Deb came forward near her and said "I, Shri Deb Roy, angiras gotra, from this time onwards at the holy place of Puri keep Krishna and Rukmini as *Sakshi* an outing *kumkum* on Aarashi's forehead and I promise to love her, protect her and honor her till my last breath. The priest there started laughing thinking Deb had put up a good show.

Aarashi was still with mixed emotions. She was also happy because at last she would have at least one person to call her own and then she could have her own family. But still, she had not answered "yes" for marrying Deb.

This was all Deb's excitement; he assumed it was a YES when she waved to him from the balcony, the other night when he dropped her home and sent her that proposing text. Then in the evening, they went to *Sakshi* Gopal temple which was 40 km from Puri. The temple is of old architecture. But the most attractive thing there is Krishna standing with his flute.

No one can explain in words what that kind of beauty has, no adjectives are enough. But one thing is for sure; whoever goes in the vicinity of Krishna, surely falls in love with him. There is no doubt about it.

A tall black statue with red alta on the leg and big silver anklets, you can't lift your eyes beyond the legs only, and then imagine how beautiful the face would be.

They entered the temple and Deb held Aarashi closely and said Mrs. Aarashi Deb Roy, I love you and will keep loving you till I die. See I am saying this in front of *Sakshi*

Gopal, and she just smiled and said let's go back, it will be late, she held herself back from saying "I love you too Deb".

After meeting her beloved Krishna in Puri in *Sakshi* Gopal she was very happy.

On the way back, Deb asked, "So, Mrs. Roy, how did you like our marriage? Well, it was not very lavish, but it was in God's court.

Aarashi sounded a little irritated and asked what this Mrs. Roy was? all the time, huh? Deb, fun is ok sometimes but not always. Life has already made fun of me, but that was less so now you have started this new fun of marriage.

Deb said, "Arashi, this is not fun at all, I had told you, I want to marry, and at Rukmini Mata temple when the priest said put *sindoor* (vermilion) I took it as an omen from lord Jagannath for our marriage and also in front of *Sakshi* Gopal I told you I will love you, protect you, honor you till I die. This all is no fun to me Arashi.

Arashi said oh ok. Lord Jagannath gave me an omen and even *Sakshi* Gopal was witness to all this. Now I will come to your house as Mrs. Aarashi Deb Roy when they come and give me witness of my marriage. Aarashi challenged Deb.

Deb's heart was shattered. He didn't speak a word throughout the journey, till he reached Howrah. There too they went their own separate ways. No phone calls, no text messages, nothing. Both were back to their gloomy days.

Deb was praying to Krishna that Jagannath, you know I had no bad intentions. I really love Aarshi and intend to marry her. How will I get you to give witness?

Aarashi was blaming herself. She was guilty because she knew, she would never get any better guy than Deb, but after years her family had got in touch with her and her father kept ill, she needed to send money to her ill father as well as her sister's education, she was afraid that now if she does something nasty, she will lose her family forever.

Little did she know that sacrificing love would give her more pain and the family was back in touch because her father's income had stopped; they needed money. Not Arashi. Aarashi did not understand this.

The following morning Aarashi woke up early and decided to visit Dakishneshwar Kali temple. She wanted to ask for forgiveness for being rude to Deb and breaking his heart. It was winter so she was wearing jeans and a heavy jacket with a scarf. She went to the Kali temple.

She prayed there for a while. She asked her Goddess mother to give her strength to fight through life and went to obeisance to Shivalinga from there she came to the little Ladoo Gopal mandir meaning Krishna temple.

There she kneeled down to pray, and she felt a hand over her head giving her *ashirwad* (blessing) saying

"*Sada suhagan rahi dudho nano puto phalo*". (Always stay happy with children).

After taking the *ashirwad*, she saw nobody around her, only a mild fragrance of sandalwood was in the air. It took her a few seconds to understand what had just happened. She looked at herself doubting if she was in a sari, no she was in jeans. She thought, "What the hell was that"?

She looked inside the temple and there she found Gopal giving a naughty smile and asking, "How many more witnesses do you want"?

Aarashi could not stop her tears of happiness.

She realised that it was a divine blessing from Gopal, the deity she had been praying to for years. Aarashi felt overwhelmed with gratitude and joy, knowing that her prayers had been heard and answered. Don't doubt true love, it is like offering water to your beloved deity, so pure and serene that God will have to intervene to bring those two souls close to each other so that they merge into one.

This is Aarashi's emotional journey from doubt to belief in the power of true love and divine intervention. The significance of Gopal, the deity, in Aarashi's life and how her prayers were answered at the temple.

Sometimes we need faith in something greater than ourselves to bring us closer to our true purpose or happiness in life.

VERMILION EXTENSION:

In India, we have the culture of writing shrimati (Mrs.) before writing shri (Mr). Women are considered Laxmi, and husbands are considered Vishnu. Laxmi and Vishnu, Parvati and Shivji, the celestial couples, are worshipped in every house. The divorce rate in our country was very low in the past few decades, but the scenario is quite different now. What could have escalated the divorce rate in our country in these few years? The reasons are so many that they cannot be counted on fingers. What I think is why the divorce rates have increased; I will write about it in the coming paragraphs. But first, see what makes a marriage successful.

A successful marriage requires mutual respect, effective communication, and a strong foundation of trust. In recent years, societal changes such as increased financial independence of women, changing gender roles, and evolving attitudes towards divorce may have contributed to the rise in divorce rates.

In the above paragraph, I mentioned other gods but not Lord Krishna because Lord Krishna is worshipped with his beloved. Lord Krishna is the embodiment of love himself. I wanted to narrate a small story that I had heard from my grandmother when I was small and hardly understood the deeper meaning of the story. The story goes like this: Lord Krishna had eight wives: Rukmini, Satyabhama, Jambavati, Kalindi, Mitravinda, Nagnajiti, Bhadra, and Lakshmana. We mainly know about two of them, Rukmini and Satyabhama. Satyabhama was always envious of Rukmini. She wanted to prove that she loved Krishna more than Rukmini, so she decided she would weigh Krishna with all her gold and show the world how much she loved Krishna. She made Lord sit on one side of the weighing scale, and on the other, she started bringing and pouring her gold ornaments. She kept on pouring and pouring, but Lord Krishna wasn't lifted by an inch. Satyabhama started sweating and getting anxious. More gold was bought, but still, there was no change. Then Satyabhama went running to Rukmini and told her the whole thing that was going on. Lord Krishna was sitting silently with the same mesmerising smile on his face. Rukmini understood the whole thing and told Satyabhama to take a tulsi leaf and place it over a heap of gold with love. Satyabhama took a tulsi leaf and placed it over her gold without ego and with total surrender to her husband, and to her surprise, the weighing scale was lifted just by the weight of a tulsi leaf. No, no, sorry, not the weight of a tulsi leaf; it was the weight of love, the weight of surrendering, the weight of respect, the weight of being egoless. It was a lesson learned for Satyabhama that material wealth could never outweigh the value of love and humility. From that day on, she cherished the tulsi leaf more than any amount of gold. Yes, being egoless has weight. That's called the weight of being responsible.

This should be the kind of relationship between a husband and a wife. Egoless first, and then love and surrender will come naturally in a relationship. It's not for women only; it's for both partners equally. Then only there can be a beautiful relationship, just like our old generations had. My father's sister (my aunty) got angry when she heard about fights between couples. She would say that our generations were such that when our kolhapuri chappal would tear, we would go to a cobbler and get it mended, but we never thought of buying a new one, not because we didn't have money but because we cared about what we owned. We took care of what belonged to us. And now you people have become so heartless that you have a new sandal today, and tomorrow you want a new one because you get bored that fast. Your generation doesn't value anything. You consider nothing to belong to you, and you belong to no one, be it human or non-human. And yes, she was right.

Today's generation has become commitment-phobic. They prefer instant gratification and constant change, never truly appreciating the value of what they have. It's a shame that the concept of loyalty and care for belongings seems to be fading away in today's society. Now I am sharing (as a counselling psychologist) the reason why the divorce rate has increased so much. First and foremost, the reason is that they have impossible expectations of each other as a couple. When the two of them fall in love, it is all about coffee dates, movies, shopping, and long phone calls. Nothing is wrong with that. But when they get married, reality comes and starts staying with them. They realise that marriage requires compromise, communication, and hard work, which can be a rude awakening for some. Additionally, societal pressures and changing norms may also contribute to the increase in divorce rates as individuals struggle to maintain a sense of self within the confines of a relationship. They, as a couple, need to realise that every day they need to fall in love with each other again. Yesterday's love was a little less; today they need to love each other a little more, and tomorrow again a little more. Each day, I fall in love with the same person, forgetting and forgiving the fight I had last night.

Also, couples are missing trust in their relationship. As a wife, I trust that if something happens to me, I can fully depend on my husband. Trust that my wife supports me in all my decisions, even if I may fail sometimes if I take some risks in life. Here, couples sometimes think of themselves first. What about my financial security? What about my mental health? What about my parents? If, as a couple, we have both accepted each other completely, where does this come from?

In Hindu tradition, we have a ritual called saptapadi, where the bride and groom take seven vows, keeping fire as a witness to these vows. Nowadays, no one explains these vows to newlyweds. The vows are as follows:

1. Let us stay in good health and carry out our duties and responsibilities to each other.

2. Let us both develop our mental and spiritual powers.

3. Let us increase our wealth and comfort by righteous and proper means.

4. Let us acquire knowledge, happiness, and harmony through mutual love, respect, and trust.

5. Let us be blessed with a contended family of strong, virtuous, and heroic children.

6. Let us be blessed with long lives.

7. Let us remain true companions, committed only to each other.

Let us pass this on to the future generation and make them understand what mutual love, understanding, and trust mean.

Here are a few questions for newlywed couples looking to strengthen their bond and build a solid foundation for their future together.:

1. One way to further elaborate on the concept of mutual love, understanding, and trust is by discussing how communication plays a crucial role in building and maintaining these aspects within a relationship.

2. Another angle to explore could be examining different cultural or societal perspectives on what constitutes mutual love, understanding, and trust, shedding light on how these values may vary across different backgrounds.

3. It would also be interesting to delve into the impact that past experiences and traumas can have on one's ability to give and receive mutual love, understanding, and trust in relationships.

4. Building upon the idea of trust within relationships, an exploration of how vulnerability and openness contribute to deepening connections between partners could provide valuable insights for readers seeking to strengthen their own bonds.

5. Lastly, considering the role of self-love and personal growth in fostering mutual love, understanding, and trust.

SAKHI

There is a destiny that makes us brothers: no one goes his way alone. All that we send into the lives of others comes back into our own. Edwin Markham

Humans are social animals. We are here on the planet to learn and spread love and compassion to all other beings. So, the karma that one performs can never be individual; it is shared karma or group karma. This makes the concept of karma very difficult to grasp because not only many people are involved, but also many births are involved.

One cannot get things before the destined time, and destiny will decide. "Waqt se pahele, naseeb se jyada kuch nahi milta." Common karma attracts individuals to each other. For example, I would like to narrate a small story:

There was a bus going on a pilgrimage. The bus was full. All the devotees were singing devotional songs and chanting, enjoying the journey. But as the bus started climbing the mountains, the rain started pouring like cats and dogs. The passengers all got scared. The driver halted the bus at one place and said he couldn't go any further unless we decided. All were curious to know what that was.

The driver said, I have travelled on this route for years but never had such a situation. The thunder and rain are such that surely, we all may die. I am sure there is a sinner on this bus whom God doesn't want to come near HIM. All the other passengers looked at each other and nodded in agreement. But the question was: how do you find out who the sinner was?

After a lot of discussion, they came up with a solution. Far away, there was a huge tree. One person had to leave the bus, walk out of the bus, stand under the tree for a minute, then come back, walking slowly. If he is a sinner, he will be struck by lightning. All the passengers agreed on this. No one had any objections. All agreed in unison.

The testing for the sinner started. With the driver going first, he came back victorious. Slowly, one by one, passengers started going, chanting God's name on their lips but deep down in their hearts, remembering all the sins they had committed. As soon as they got back alive to the bus, they believed they were the supreme bhakta (devotee) of God, and all their sins were excused.

Finally, only one man remained on the bus who was left to pass the test. Before he even stepped out, people started cursing him. Ohhhh, you are the sinner. We should have recognised you long ago.

"See, as your turn came, it stopped raining too." "Because of you, we all would have died; thanks to the driver, he came up with such a good idea." The poor man was really hurt, but he didn't utter a word because he was on a pilgrimage and he had full faith in his God.

He stepped off the bus and started walking towards the tree. There was a huge, thunderous sound. All were convinced that it was him. Till they would take a breath of sigh, the lightning fell on the bus, and the man had hardly reached the tree. This is how complicated karma is. Had the man been on the bus, they were all safe.

They were all sinners except the man. "Vinash kale vipreet buddhi" (when destruction time is near, one goes against the brain). Their time was over, so they were forced to get him off the bus.

Group karmas and family karmas are so complex that they go on for lifetimes together.

"Phoolon ka taron ka sabka kehna hai, Ek hazaaron mein meri behna hai ", this song was sung by younger sister Veera to elder sister Divya. Being brought up in a well-to-do and traditional family where the expectation for male children is higher, children like Veera can feel that

they are unwanted in some way or another. In a joint family, grandmothers and aunts tend to say over and over that instead of her, if it were a male child, all the trouble would be over.

Maybe the child not only hears it but will also store it as a trauma somewhere in their body and manifest it later in his or her life. The feeling of being unwanted or hearing from elders that he or she is worthless is a permanent wound for young minds. But Veera had an older sister, Divya, who was more than a sister to her. She was seven years older than her. Divya felt as if God had sent an angel into her life; there was a reason for that. Veera's birthday was the next day of Divya's, so Divya felt she was a gift sent by God.

Now Divya had all the reason to believe more in her God and in her angel too. She took very good care of Veera. Even when she started going to school, Divya would hold her hand, drop her off at class, during lunch break feed her with her own hands, get her back home, take her studies, do her own studies, and put her to bed. She was almost her second mom. Her mom didn't bother much about Veera, but she did about Divya.

Years went by. Both were growing up. Divya took up medical studies, and Veera took up engineering. Now the roles are reversed. By now, cell phones were just new in the market (although WhatsApp was not yet introduced). Veera grew up as a bold and independent individual, while Divya was shy and introverted. Many times, when Divya would plan to go out for a coffee with friends, her mom would not object, but Veera would ask, "Dee, where are you going?

With whom and how many friends are there? By what time will you return? Should I come with you?" Divya would get irritated and say noooooo. When mom would say, Why are you troubling her? Veera would say, Maa, she is very naive; she doesn't understand anything. If anyone speaks sweetly to her, she will melt. Her mom said, Let her do whatever she wants. You don't interfere. Her life is her choice.

Within a few months, Divya got married. It was a love marriage. Veera said she doesn't like that boy because he is taking you away from me. For Veera, it was like she was losing her mother. For the past 22 years, they had been celebrating their birthdays together, and now that would stop. Still, a few of their friends didn't know their correct birthdates.

The first few months were very difficult for both. The calls were not free. Divya loved writing letters, so she wrote letters and posted them. They called each other twice a week. Soon, both Divya and Veera had good news to share.

Divya called up Veera and asked where her pet snoop was. Veera said it was playing. Veera asked why she was asking for the pet, and Divya said that Snoop was going to become mama soon; there was a long pause till Veera understood what it meant. Later, she screamed with joy and asked if she was really going to be Maasi.

Divya said yes. Veera started crying loudly. She could not hold back the tears. She was very happy. She said, Dee, see you call me Angel, na? No, your baby is an angel; you know I am selected to go to Egypt. The chances were very slim. I wanted to give you this good news. Now I know whom to shop for. Both were so much at peace. These are the moments of bliss.

Veera came from Egypt and found no one at home. Then she called Divya, even though she was not picking up the call. Veera thought of calling up her dad, but the phone rang. Dad said they were at the hospital, and he couldn't speak right now. Veera had to wait to know what had happened. When her mom came in the evening, she told me that Divya had lost the baby due to some complications.

Veera could not believe her ears. She was heartbroken. She didn't understand what to do. She sat down for a while, composed herself, and started hiding the stuff she had purchased for the baby from Egypt. She didn't want Divya to look at it and cry.

When Divya was brought home, she was very depressed. Veera and Snoop did not leave her for a second. Always fooling around her as she sat on the chair, Snoop climbed on her lap and slept. He was a pup. That brought her a lot of peace.

A few months later, Divya underwent another abortion. This was traumatic for the entire family. The specialist was consulted. Treatments were taken. From Ayurveda to homoeopathy—anything anybody suggests—the family was ready to try. There was too much tension in the family regarding Divya's condition.

Physically, emotionally, and mentally, she was losing control. It has been almost nine years since her marriage. When the world points fingers at you, your education will not come to rescue you. Being childless is not a crime.

Anyway, after genetic tests and all other treatments were started in Mumbai, Veera's parents were looking for a groom for Veera. They liked one, and talks were going on. Veera wanted to ask Divya for her opinion, but she decided not to trouble her as she was already in trouble. Without giving much thought, Veera gave consent.

It was an engagement morning, and when Divya heard Veera arguing with someone, she got out of bed. Divya asked who it was and what was happening. Veera had tears in her eyes and said it was her fiancée, and he was arguing over something. Then Divya got a little serious and said, Look, Veera, no one is forcing this marriage on you; if you are not happy, let's call it off now. You are not even engaged. If you want, I will speak to Dad. Do you want me to speak? Veera said, "No, Dee, I will handle it.".

After a few days, there was good news that Divya was pregnant again. This time, the utmost care was taken. Meanwhile, Veera was married. Things changed. After marriage, Veera hardly spoke to Divya. Divya used to call her; she used to be busy with work or with in-laws.

Divya started feeling that marriage changed Veera. Maybe she is no more important to her than she was before.

She had expected that at the time of delivery, Veera would be with her, but Divya was disappointed when she got to know that she had chosen to go to the Andaman Islands. Divya felt all the love Veera had for her had changed after Veera's marriage, and priorities changed after marriage. She kept all these feelings to herself and did not tell them to her mom or dad.

Finally, on Monday afternoon, a beautiful angel was born. Divya's mom and husband were with her in the hospital. After staying in the hospital for three days, when she returned home, she screamed in joy when she saw Veera standing in front of her. Divya forgot about her baby and hugged Veera so tightly, and both cried till their hearts were light like a feather. Divya could just manage to ask "How" or "When," and Veera replied, "Morning, forever."".

Nobody understood anything. Mom kept the baby in a cradle. Veera started telling her what happened after marriage. Veera said, Mom, Dee, I thought I was a very strong and independent girl, and true, I am. But these qualities are never enough. Even the circumstances should be favourable.

I am saying this because you heard me have an argument with my fiancée on engagement day. I am sure I would have legally dragged him to court, but the turn of events was not in my favor. The moment he knew you were pregnant, he took advantage; he started hitting me and abusing me. If I complained at home, there would be a big deal out of it.

Police cases or maybe fights—you don't know what—would give you more stress. I did not want you to lose this baby because of me. It's better to stay with a demon for nine months than to lose an angel after nine months.

Divya held Veera's hand and said, Tell me, how can I repay you this favour?

This is eternal bonding. One comes to protect the other.

SAKHI EXTENSION

Humans are called social animals, and that is for a reason. Since humans were cavemen, they always lived in groups. There are many reasons why humans have social relationships. In the old days, families were bigger and things were different. India is an agricultural country, where the majority of a family's occupation was agriculture, and parents did not mind having many children, as the son of the family would help in the occupation. Bringing up the children was also not a big challenge, as the family was joint with all the uncles, aunts, grandmothers, and grandfathers. Children received love from all. There seemed to be no distinction for children, as they treated all their aunts like their moms. This close-knit family structure fostered strong social bonds and a sense of community among relatives. As societies have evolved and become more individualistic, the dynamics of social relationships have shifted, leading to smaller family units and different forms of social connections.

MINDING YOUR OWN BUSINESS

"I heard this story about a fish. He swims up to this older fish and says, I'm trying to find this thing they call the ocean. 'The ocean ?' says the older fish. 'That's what you're in right now.' 'This?'says the young fish. .' This is water. What I want is the ocean."

Soul.

Imagine you have wanted and prayed for something from God for years, and God finally gave it to you silently. You have it, but still, you are not aware of it, just like the little fish in the story above. What are your emotions towards this? Will you be angry with yourself? Calling yourself foolish. Or will you have pity on yourself for asking the foolish big fish and go and ask someone else and try again? Are all the prayers that we want to come true really worth coming true? What if all our prayers come true? Will we be confident that we will have a life without sorrow? Think over this as I am narrating my past life story, which I saw through regression sessions.

This life, I am very fortunate to have been born into a middle-class family with nothing much to complain about. As a family, we had the same challenges as every other family. Apart from that, I was doing well in education, and my parents were proud of me as everyone else is. I was nothing extraordinary. Until one day in September 2010, an extraordinary event took place in my life. It was a Sunday afternoon, and I was taking my beauty nap when suddenly I had an urge to pick up a paper and pen. I am a poet, so I thought maybe because of that I was feeling so. But no, this was something different. I tried to brush this thought aside multiple times, but in vain. Finally, I woke up and took my diary and pen. And as I held the pen, it started scribbling as if I had started writing for the first time. The pen was not at all in my control. I was scared like hell. But I could hear a voice in my head saying, "I do not want to do this; stop it."

30-year-old me, alone at home on that Sunday afternoon. After this happened, I locked my flat and went and sat in a café coffee day till my husband arrived home. I was confused as to whether to share this with him or not; he must not think I was going crazy because of my work pressure. I decided not to tell him. I told no one. But I noticed that whenever I held the pen, that thought came rushing: "No, I don't want to do this.". I used to think to myself, I am a lecturer, and I must write, if my hand does not write, I will be thrown out of college,so now you better cooperate.

Years went by, and I almost forgot about it. During COVID, I went through my past life regression. I remembered this episode, and I was curious to know what that was all about.

After sitting still for a few minutes and slowly going into the trace (well, I have learned past life regression), the past flashed in front of my eyes. I could see a place with big, steep mountains. It was not a modern era. I tried to find the place; it was Tibet. Below the mountains were green fields. It was a tiny village. It was a happy village. I was searching for myself in the village, but I did not find myself. I saw my house, which was a small hut. (Here, I means consciousness), but nobody lived there apart from me and my dead parents' paintings. Right in front of my house, I had my fields, which looked green, which means I must be taking very good care of them. Then my consciousness took me to the top of the mountain.

There was a cave there. I used to climb that mountain daily before sunrise and sit for meditation. When my parents died of illness and I became an orphan, I climbed up and came to this cave to cry my heart out. I was only 8 then. Now I am around 28. Here I found my master, who taught me meditation and martial arts. Even so, he left me and went towards the Himalayas. But he has asked me to continue with my meditation practice. So daily I climb the mountain twice.

There was a long pause as I was not saying anything (my consciousness was seeing something interesting). We moved a little further in time and saw that my hut was filled with people from the village as well as other villages. They have come to ask for solutions to their problems. As there was a rumour in the village that one early morning BUDDHA himself had come to bless me, and few villagers were witnesses to this, from that day onwards I was treated like I carried the message of God to the villagers, whereas I was unaware of this story behind my back. I went to the mountains, did my meditations, and whatever questions the villagers asked, I would ask Buddha for the answer, and whatever he told me in meditation, I would come and tell them. I did not ask anything in return except one day, as I was walking down the mountain, I saw my field burning, my hut on fire, and people gathered in front of my house screaming, "We will kill you, you fraud. You said it would rain on certain days. We ploughed the fields. Where are the rains? Come down, we will kill you.".

I got so scared that I went running back to the cave and hid myself in a corner where I couldn't be seen. I spent days there without food and without water, saying to myself that I would never pass on God's messages to anyone. And that was the promise I had made before I gave up my life as a monk in Tibet.

This samskara is deeply rooted in my brain. The incident that happened in September 2010 was not out of the blue. During that time, I was going through a lot of stress. Just 10 days ago in August, I had my second miscarriage, and I was blaming God and constantly asking him questions. Nonstop. I asked him if I deserved this and all these immature questions. So, this samskara of past life was trying to take his hood out and calm me down, but again, it did not even want to break the owe taken during death.

Same me, same soul, same troubles—so close to God yet so far. In the ocean, searching for water. Why am I saying this?

When you do bhakti, or meditation, or, in that case, any sadhana of any god or goddess, you will get siddhis very easily. It becomes very easy to make predictions about other people. It becomes easy to tell the personalities of other people whom you don't even know, to predict lottery numbers, and many other things. But once the Sadhak gets entangled in this and starts enjoying the fame and praise, he will forget why he started in the first place. There will be no place for God in all this. So, I said, if you start praying and all your prayers start being answered, then you will be God. You will have no one to be grateful for. In average life, we only live an ungrateful and ignorant life. Imagine when God starts granting our wishes.

Obsessing over other people's lives requires you to abandon your own. You have limited time and energy; use it for your growth, not to mentally exit a stranger's highlight reel.

Minding my own business is the most powerful move I've ever made. I never realised how studying other people's

lives took so much valuable time away from my own...
Until I shifted my focus back to my own sh*t.

Then I began to really thrive.

Your life requires your attention.

WHY AM I TELLING YOU ALL THIS?

The other day, I came across an advertisement for the Apple Eye Gear Pro. It's an eye gear where we just have to wear the device on the eyes, and it teleports us to a different world. The features the eye gear has are so amazing, as they have advertised, that, according to the company, you don't need any humans around you. The device will turn your images into life-size photos. With eye movement, you can select and talk to anyone sitting miles away, just like he or she is in front of you. But in the end, it's only you and the eye gear in the house. Is this all a human need? While the technology may offer incredible capabilities, it's important to consider the potential consequences of isolating oneself from human interaction. Finding a balance between virtual and real-world experiences is essential for overall well-being and social connection.

I am extremely concerned about the coming generations, as already with the nuclear family, we have made our children far from grandparents, uncles, and aunts (not on purpose, of course), no matter how much we may love them. Ok, we will say that's because of financial reasons. We have decided to have smaller families with only one child, but technology is intruding into our lives, and we are inviting it with wide open arms. All I want to say is that humans will always need other humans. Love and care cannot be shown and felt through gadgets. Technology is meant for our convenience, but it has replaced all our emotions.

Imagine sitting beside a friend when she is sad; you just place your hand on her cheeks, or you are worried about something, and your dad gives you a tight hug and says, "Be brave." Won't there be tears in the corner of your eyes? The same goes for love and compassion. Love and compassion can't be sent to one place. We need to reach out.

Relationships are the most important part of human life. That makes life more worth living. It gives us strength and sense, and it gives us a chance to reflect on who we are as a person. In relationships, I mean all sorts, from family to friends, everybody as we interact as a person. Relationships are not always positive and happy; some can be sour and ugly. But they are such for a reason. Maybe they want to teach us some lessons or some karmic bondage that we must go through. But still, we have a choice: accept relationships as they are. If things are not being accepted by the other person, just let them be. Don't make it much uglier by messing up word for word..

Mother's love cannot be replaced. Fathers' care cannot be replaced. Sisters' little sacrifices cannot be replaced. Brothers' support cannot be replaced. Family is an irreplaceable bond that provides unconditional love and support. Cherishing these relationships can bring immense joy and fulfillment to our lives.

Let's try as mindful humans to keep technology a little away and relearn to bond back with the relationships that are still there. Let's water the relationship with attention and care, and the tree of life will bloom with flowers of love and happiness. Let's make an effort to prioritise our relationships and nurture them with love and care. By investing time and effort into our family bonds, we can create lasting memories and experiences that will bring us closer together.

HOW TO WIN AT LIFE

Step 1: Let people do what they need to do to make them happy, mind their own business, and do what you need to do to make you happy.

THE END.

AHAM BRAHMASMI

The term MESSIAH complex sounds out of context at first; it's like a mismatched pair, not made for each other. Yes, MESSIAH COMPLEX is complex to understand, but what does this term mean? To understand that, we will first understand the human beings that God has created.

Every person has an "I "inside them, which separates him/her from another person. This "I" is known as the EGO of the person. Each person builds his/her personality around this ego. His/her life revolves around this ego alone. The ego is like an identity that introduces me to myself, to put it in simple language. It's like looking in the mirror, it's not present, but we identify ourselves with it, and we spend our whole life protecting it, serving it, and sometimes even inflating it.

We are living in an era that is full of confusion. That is because we never asked appropriate questions to our elders, we did what we were asked to do (in other words, we obeyed them blindly), but today Gen Z is so inquisitive that they will keep asking questions till they don't get satisfactory answers to their queries, whether it be about festivals, religion, or God. They won't follow us blindly. And sometimes we fall short of answering all their questions. They are right, why should they do something without knowing the importance of it? As a friend, I will try to remove some confusion from young minds by explaining the difference between what it means to be religious and spiritual. These days, I hear many Genz saying I am a spiritual soul, an old soul. So I wonder, do they know what they mean? (I don't mean to underestimate anyone, but I just want to add a dimension to what they say.)

Being religious and being spiritual are two different aspects. They are like two faces of the same coin. Heads and tails. Let's know what being religious means.

It means following a particular religion and all the rules and regulations of that religion. If you are religious, that doesn't mean you can't be spiritual. This is wrong. "There are a thousand ways to climb a mountain, all paths lead to the same God; you choose a different path that doesn't lead you elsewhere. It will still lead you to the same almighty.". On the other hand, spirituality is more about working on ourselves and our minds. We may follow any particular religion or not; it doesn't matter. Spirituality has more to do with the spirit in ourselves, elevating the spirit to higher consciousness through meditation, different yogic ways, and breathwork. The ultimate aim is to keep one's mind calm and controlled, to carry out life in a joyful manner in this stressful world. So, whether you are religious or spiritual, you should know what your aim is for following the path that you are following.

What if we are not following any of the paths? Still, we are following a path, a path that our hearts tell us.

Some people are GOD fearing, some are God-pleasing, some are God-loving, and a few I would like to call having GOD-COMPLEX or messiah complex. I will explain this term with an example.

There was a monastery in the mountains in northern India. Teens as well as young boys from all over the world came to this monastery to become monks. As it is known, it is not so easy to be a monk. One has to give up all their belongings before entering the monastery. Also, one has to pass many levels of exams where the young monks are taught scriptures, recitations, meditations, etc. As normal people, we try to imagine, the most difficult emotion is to leave the family forever, and that is the first big hurdle. One has to cross it when one decides to become a monk, half the battle is conquered here itself.

So, in this batch of monks, there was a very bright young boy. His name was Tashi. He was determined to be a monk. He came from the nearby village of the monastery, so from when he was a toddler, this monastery always attracted him. When he became a teenager, he told his parents that he wanted to become a monk and give up his family life. Being the only son, hearing their son's words, their hearts sank. But he was determined. Their parents tried to convince him in whatever way possible. They failed miserably. They bought him a lamb so that he could fall in love with it, take care of it, and maybe change the decision, but no, he was firm. The day came when he finally walked towards the monastery, leaving behind his parents crying, and the lamb, which his parents had to take care of now.

Tashi has passed the first big hurdle that makes a normal person weaker, which is to give up the family. ATTACHMENT. He was so focused that he did not have to go through a lot of emotional turmoil. He was easily detached from the family, whereas other students' detachment from the family is the most difficult part. After coming to the monastery, they get homesick; they miss their parents; they miss their belongings; and they miss their pets, if they have any. It takes months to adjust to the new environment, and until they make some good friends who help them miss their home a little less.

Education started, all the students had to shave their heads (even though this is a form of detaching oneself from the image of how they look), and recitations were done. They had to wake up before the sunrise. The boy, Tashi, was looking forward to what was coming next, he was so impatient and eager to learn. He was a bright student. Days passed by, and with each day there was an increase in everyone's knowledge. Tashi, especially because he was taking it differently, treated himself differently from others. He was a fast learner; considered others as nothing in front of him. He felt other students were dumb, and they did not understand what the masters taught as much as Tashi understood the subject. Tashi had an opinion about every student in his mind, and he would rush to teach them even if they did not ask for help. The first few times the other boys welcomed the help with gratitude but later Tashi "forced the help" upon everybody without being asked, thinking, "I am always right and you should all listen to me." This becomes a type of messiah syndrome. In a sense, Tashi started thinking of himself as a messiah of the students. Without me these students are nothing. If I am not around, they will be lost. He also forgot that masters were there to guide the other students. Somehow this news went to one of the master's ears. Master decided to open Tashi's eyes.

The next day, the master took all the students by the lake for meditation. Before he gave the instructions for meditation, he called Tashi in front of all the students and appreciated him for his hard work and his intelligence, also mentioned how grateful he is that he goes and helps all the other students without being asked. All applauded for Tashi. Then the master said that as a reward, Tashi would sit in the green boat for meditation, which is anchored, Tashi went running towards the boat. Similarly, the master assigned other places for other students on the land so that they could meditate for a while and later all have to share their experiences. The master was closely observing Tashi.

Tashi was sitting in the boat, which was on the water. He sat in the middle, closed his eyes, and started with his meditation. After some time passed, he went into deep meditation. Suddenly, the waters were turbulent, and the neighbouring empty boats started dashing Tashi's boat. Initially, Tashi was calm and composed, but later irritation started showing on his face. His master was observing him from afar. Initially, Tashi tried to ignore the disturbance caused by the turbulence of the boat, but slowly that irritation started growing into anger. His eyebrows started to shrink, and his face turned red. Tashi finally lost control and shouted," Who is that idiot who is trying to interrupt my meditation?". His master, who was observing him, said, " Tashi, open your eyes.". When Tashi opened his eyes, he found no one in the neighbouring boats. The turbulence was because of waves, whereas Tashi thought that someone from his class was playing a prank on him, and usually he wanted to excel. Finally, when he couldn't control it, he burst out in anger.

Tashi's master called Tashi and asked him to share his experience. Tashi said that when I started to meditate, I was feeling very calm and quiet. But later, I started feeling irritated because somebody was trying to break my meditation. Then a chain of thoughts started entering my mind: how can my classmates be so cruel? I helped them so much, and now they are spoiling my meditation. I am being so good to them, and in return, they are giving me this. Do I deserve this type of treatment? They should treat me differently. But when I opened my eyes, I saw there was no one there. All my thoughts went in vain.

Master asked Tashi: Do you understand the meaning of these thoughts that arose in your mind?

Tashi said, Yes, but master, will you explain?

Master gathered all the class and explained to everyone:

The master said that the first thing to remember is that if you are feeling disturbed, find out where that thought is coming from. Is it in your mind, or is someone else responsible? Tashi always felt someone else was responsible for his disturbance, but it was his mind and thoughts, so when stressed or upset, always ask your mind, What's the problem? Tashi immediately started counting the favors he had done for others.

Master asked Tashi, "Tashi, have any of these students ever come to you to ask for help or advice?"

Tashi said, "No."

The master said, "Then why did you become their messiah? They would have survived without you, don't you think?"

Master continued, Being a messiah is not wrong, Tashi; what is wrong is carrying the ego with it. Either you are an angel or you are a human with an ego; you can't be both. Today, you saw what your ego did to you. Little turbulence of water made you question whether you deserved to be treated like this by your classmates. When you were not even sure if they were present there or not. But you assumed that it must be your classmates because you have done them a favour, and now you hold the right to hold a grudge against them. You did not think, even for a moment, that if it could be your master testing you, because your ego has told you that you are the best and you know when you are the best, why will your master test you?

This is called the messiah syndrome, where one wants to sacrifice one's life for the betterment of others; maybe others have asked for it or not; it's not important. It's mostly seen in Indian women, who sacrifice their education, their jobs, their social life, their happiness, their friendships, etc. in the name of bringing up their children and giving them full attention. These mothers work hard so that their children study well and someday settle abroad. And finally, when that day arrives after 20 years, they feel the nest is empty. All that they sacrificed was for whom and what? Husband is busy with his own work. Now children have left the nest, they have no friends or social circle, nor are they good at gadgets, the thought creeps in... Do I deserve this? I have to stay all alone. Weren't you the same mother who sacrificed your entire youth for your child, had he asked for it? You should know where and how to strike the balance. After all, you also had a life.

Either do it without expectation, be happy that you did what you did, or don't do it at all.